WINNING MODERN WARS

WINNING MODERN WARS

*Iraq, Terrorism,
and the American Empire*

GENERAL WESLEY K. CLARK
U.S. Army (Retired)

PublicAffairs *New York*

Book design by Mark McGarry, Texas Type & Book Works
Set in Minion

Library of Congress Cataloging-in-Publication Data
Clark, Wesley K.
Winning modern wars: Iraq, terrorism, and the American Empire / Wesley K. Clark
p. cm.
Includes bibliographical references and index.
ISBN 1–58648–218–1
1. Iraq War, 2003. 2. War on Terrorism, 2001–
3. United States—Foreign relations—2001–
4. United States—Military policy.
5. Imperialism. I. Title
DS79.76.C58 2003
956.7044'3–dc22
2003062342

FIRST EDITION
10 9 8 7 6 5 4 3 2 1

*This book is dedicated to the men and women
of the United States armed forces and their families,
who together have answered their country's call.
Theirs is a lasting legacy.*

CONTENTS

INTRODUCTION

ON APRIL 9, 2003, in a scene replayed time and again on televisions across the world, a U.S. Marine hooked up a cable from his armored vehicle and, with Iraqis standing nearby, pulled down the large statue of Saddam Hussein in Baghdad. It was a hugely symbolic act, the toppling of a tyrant, and the fulfillment of President Bush's longstanding aim of regime change in Baghdad. The symbolism seemed even richer when it later emerged that the Marines had first given the Iraqis a rope, then had to do it themselves with the armored vehicle. The United States had pushed, encouraged, and prompted for years. Now, with American steel directly engaged, and with the U.S. leading, it was done, even if fighting might last for a few more days.

I had watched and participated in that struggle in various positions from the very beginning. In late July 1990, as the Iraqi divisions began to mass on the border to invade Kuwait, I was in command of the U.S. Army's National Training Center at Fort Irwin, California, in the middle of the Mojave Desert. A brigade from Major General Barry McCaffrey's 24th Infantry Division, designated among the first to be called in case of war in the Persian Gulf, was visiting with us to undergo operational training. "We will deploy," said McCaffrey, "and if we fight, we'll win." Subsequently his division did indeed deploy and went on to earn distinction in the brief ground war. My request to leave my command and deploy, however, was rebuffed immediately; I remained at Fort Irwin, where we developed tactics to breach Iraqi defenses, trained two National Guard brigades, and followed the war through the Army's intelligence and operational reporting systems.

In 1992, I was a major general commanding the 1st Cavalry Division at Fort Hood, Texas, when we deployed the first of the Operation Intrinsic Action task forces—some 1,000 troops—back to Kuwait to deter any renewed Iraqi aggression. In the mid-1990s, as Director of Strategic Plans and Policy (J–5) for the Joint Staff in the Pentagon, I helped represent the military in work with the White House and the Defense and State Departments to help develop policy toward Iraq. In the late 1990s, as a full general, serving as the commander of the U.S. European Command, I was responsible for the air operations over Iraq's northern no-fly zone. Throughout these experiences I watched the continuing flow of UN activities, received reports on Iraqi actions, participated in shaping our responses, and, above all, wondered and worried about Saddam Hussein.

During the time I was NATO's Supreme Allied Commander, Europe, however, my principal duties were associated with the Balkans. At that time we were saddled with the crisis in Kosovo that led to NATO's air campaign against the Serbs in 1999 and the subsequent peace operation in Kosovo. Through these experiences, I came to understand that a new methodology of war was emerging and that this modern war had to be prosecuted in new ways. It was enabled by high-precision air and ground combat capabilities and reflected the importance of operating with other nations in strong alliances, minimizing friendly casualties and civilian losses, and making optimum use of a battlefield almost instantly visible to the media around the world. Effectively prosecuted, modern war offered the opportunity for decisive success without having to use decisive force. In the Kosovo campaign we were able to undercut Yugoslav president Slobodan Milosevic so completely that his own people overturned his government the next year, detained him, and turned him over for trial at The Hague.

And so, as I watched the scene play out in Baghdad in April 2003, I found myself measuring the actions there against the template of modern war. What were the objectives? Had we achieved them? Had we made best use of the tools of war now available? And what were the next steps for us? Over the next four months, as I traveled around the United States and abroad, I watched as the early euphoria of American battlefield success quickly wore off. In its place was a growing concern about the current state and long-term consequences of Operation Iraqi Freedom. Saddam was no longer in power, and the Mukhabarat, the Iraqi secret police, was destroyed. As well, thousands in mass graves had been unearthed, and Iraqis were enjoying liberty and freedom of expression for the first time in more than thirty years. Still, any achievements were overshadowed by the steadily deteriorating security environment and the continuing sabotage to the reconstruction effort. The looting from the first days had been supplanted by an increasingly well organized and active guerrilla movement, capable of daily action against U.S. troops as well as occasional terrorist strikes. Worse, the U.S. forces seemed to be drawing into Iraq the very terrorists and Al

Qaeda–like organizations we had been sent there to dismantle. To add to these concerns, the press had at last begun to critically examine the evidence and analyses that had seemed to justify U.S. action in the first place. Today many are asking fundamental questions about the war against Saddam, such as whether the operation was justified, whether it has succeeded in reducing the terrorist threat we face, what precisely we are going to do in Iraq—for how long and at what cost—and how we should win the broader war against terror.

It is these questions that I hope to answer in this book. Even at this early stage in the postconflict period, some of the elements that propelled us into the war, shaped its outcome, and will determine future events in Iraq are already clear. The Bush administration has often stated that the war in Iraq must be viewed as part of the war on terror, in response to the terrible attacks on New York and the Pentagon. But the answers about the war must also be viewed from the perspective of a long pattern of U.S. involvement in the Middle East, as well as the continuing transformation of the U.S. armed forces. Moreover, the answers are connected to larger issues within the American political system—and America's role in the world.

It has been extraordinarily difficult for Americans even to ask critical questions about this war. In the aftermath of the events of 9/11, some simply sought strong American leadership and supported it without question; others feared being labeled as unpatriotic if they dared ask why. And across the breadth of America there has been a strong desire for demonstrable action to restore our sense of security. We are a resilient and tough-minded nation. Hardship unifies us. And the war on terror is tapping unused reservoirs of resolve and public-mindedness.

Still, these questions about the war need to be asked. And

they demand our best answers now, while the long-running effort against terror is still in its relatively early stages, before the course ahead is irretrievably locked in. Now, while we can still learn from our actions and their impact, and sharpen our effectiveness for the challenges ahead, and before the costs and problems associated with our actions have grown so great that change will be seen as failure and continuation will be prohibitively costly.

Chapter 1 explains the basis of our decade-long engagement with Saddam Hussein, from the Gulf War up through the first day of the conflict in March 2003, and describes the background to the American force that was dispatched. It looks at the long-standing and often revised plan for Iraq. It is a story of the interplay of our military, diplomatic, and political spheres. Visible here are some important signposts about how the use of force fits within the larger use of national power to protect our country, as well as some of the many difficulties and dilemmas faced by the military itself.

The course of the campaign dominates Chapters 2 and 3. The 2003 war in Iraq was the first full-scale test of modern war in action. That is why its lessons are so important and why there is a need to review the course of the campaign from the euphoria of the early advance, into the struggle with unexpected resistance in southern Iraq, and through the seizure of Baghdad and into subsequent occupation. War in practice is never the same as war in theory: So it proved in Iraq. Here are some of the key military elements and the basic trade-offs that shaped the outcome of the fighting, as U.S. leaders adapted their opening plan to on-the-ground reality. It was a campaign that should never have been in doubt, but in the fickle court of public opinion around the world, the significance of every tactical shift was magnified.

That, too, is the nature of modern war: Distinctive approaches to the use of public information and its consequences are as much a part of the battle plan as the troops on the ground.

Crucially, the success of the battlefield campaign, the brilliance of the tactics and leadership, and the courage of the men and women in the ranks disguised fundamental flaws in strategy. Needless risks were taken with the force structure; there was inadequate planning for the postconflict phase; and vital international support was carelessly disregarded. It has thus far been a perfect example of dominating an enemy force but failing to secure the victory.

Chapter 4 develops the analysis in the broader context, assessing the results of the war on terror to date and showing the limitations of the current efforts, at home and abroad. Although the record reveals solid achievements in the disruption of Al Qaeda, it also shows continuing threats. After 9/11, during the first months of the war on terror, a critical opportunity to nail Al Qaeda in Afghanistan was missed. Additionally our allies were neglected and a counterterrorist strategy was adopted that, despite all the rhetoric, focused the nation on a conventional attack on Iraq rather than a shadowy war against the perpetrators of the 9/11 attacks: Al Qaeda. I argue that not only did the Bush administration misunderstand the lessons of modern war, it made a policy blunder of significant proportions.

In Chapter 5 we see the continuation of the mission against Al Qaeda, and the unveiling of the "new" strategy, plus how evidence and rhetoric were used selectively to justify the decision to attack Iraq. And we see the consequences of the strategy, both in the deteriorating situation in Afghanistan and the growing postbattle conflict on the ground inside Iraq. Less than four months after dismantling Saddam's statue, we had to admit that we had

reenergized Al Qaeda by attacking an Islamic state and present-
ing terrorists with ready access to vulnerable U.S. forces. It was
the inevitable result of a flawed strategy.

Finally, in Chapter 6, I examine deeper consequences of the
policy: an all-volunteer force so committed that the U.S. Army
itself is at risk; the notion of Iraq becoming the stepping stone to
a new American Empire liberated by force of arms little more
than a fading dream. The very idea of New American Empire in
2003 shows an ignorance of the real and existing virtual empire
that America has created since the end of World War II. The failures of the strategy call for alternative prescriptions: The book
ends with mine for a more powerful but less arrogant America
abroad, and a safer and more secure America at home.

In writing this book, I have drawn a great deal on publicly
available information—news releases, press accounts, opinion
polls, speeches, testimony, and the visuals from a far-off campaign. As a military commentator during and after the war, it
was my business to follow the events closely, expressing candid
views on television and in occasional newspaper columns. But
some material is drawn from the private sources sometimes
available to retired officers, as many currently engaged in the
operations shared their thoughts and concerns. I am protecting
these sources, but the public interest demands that some of this
information be shared. Nothing in this book is derived from
classified material nor have I written anything that could compromise national security.

It wasn't my intention to write in a politically partisan manner, but rather with the same balanced analysis that I tried to
provide when I served on active duty: Call it clearly and hon-
estly; let the chips fall where they may; and take responsibility.
Nonetheless there are some strong opinions here. And as I have

become increasingly outspoken over the last year with the course of American actions in the larger campaign against terror, my commentary has sometimes been seen in partisan terms. Some in Congress and the administration sought to label my comments as politically motivated, suggesting that I had some ulterior political ambition that was driving my views. The opposite is the case: I had the views, and the views themselves brought the political attention. I believe that we need straightforward answers to questions about our policy. As I wrote the book over the summer of 2003 there was continuing speculation about whether I might engage in some manner in the 2004 election, but this looming decision had no bearing on my analysis. I recognize that people are entitled to draw their own conclusions about my motives and politics and that there will be consequences. As one of my business associates explained it to me, "Who says freedom of speech is free?"

But the real price is being paid by the men and women of our armed forces, especially the Army. Facing daily risk of attack—far from home, in an uncertain mission—they cannot and should not speak for themselves. My heart is with them in the dirty, dangerous business of combat, and with the leaders I know so well, the soldiers with whom I've served, and their families at home. Offering this analysis is the least I can do to help them and to help my country.

CHAPTER 1

GULF WAR, ROUND TWO

MARCH 20, 2003, early morning, somewhere over Iraq. The F–117 pilots checked their systems and prepared to release their 2,000-pound bombs. Behind them would follow some forty Tomahawk Sea Launched Cruise Missiles. This was no shock and awe campaign. It was to be a knockout blow aimed at only one set target: Saddam Hussein himself, his sons, and key leaders of the Iraqi regime.

Special intelligence, received only hours before in Washington, indicated that Saddam Hussein and his senior leaders, probably including his sons, would gather briefly at a house on the southern outskirts of Baghdad. A successful attack might yield a "clean win" for the United States. Even a near-miss would certainly represent a heavy psychological blow to Saddam.

The strike went in right on target, followed by the missiles. It was a smart, gritty response to unexpected intelligence. And it showed a remarkably agile and confident integrated Air Force and Navy effort. But it wasn't the real beginning of the war.

The truth is, the war with Iraq began in early January 1991—

with the congressional resolution authorizing President George H. W. Bush to use military force to liberate Kuwait—and the war hasn't ended yet.

In August of 1990, Iraq invaded and overran its smaller neighbor, Kuwait (see map). U.S. policy at the time was to contain any further Iraqi aggression, force an Iraqi withdrawal, and liberate Kuwait. As the first President Bush announced, "This will not stand." Through five months of diplomacy and threat in the autumn of 1990, the American public saw in Iraqi president Saddam Hussein a Middle East potentate who was thoroughly dislikable. Arrogant, threatening, deceitful, he became the arch-villain in a thirteen-year morality play starring the United States.

A massive coalition was assembled, and United Nations (UN) authority was gained to require Saddam to pull his forces out of Kuwait. When he ultimately refused, the military campaign against him began on January 17, 1991. A thirty-nine-day air campaign preceded combined air and ground operations aimed at cutting off and destroying Iraqi forces in Kuwait. But the American successes were so overwhelming that operations were halted after only about 100 hours of ground combat. At the time it seemed we had won a magnificent victory, but many of the Iraqi forces, particularly the Republican Guards, were not destroyed. An uneasy peace followed, with the Iraqi air force restricted from flying in newly established "no-fly zones" and Iraqi pledges to the UN to give up their weapons of mass destruction—or WMD, which includes chemical, biological, and nuclear weapons—in order to achieve the lifting of UN-imposed sanctions.

Back in the United States a few months later, victory parades in New York City and down Constitution Avenue in Washington capped an incredible surge of patriotism and support for the incumbent president, as well as for the American armed forces and

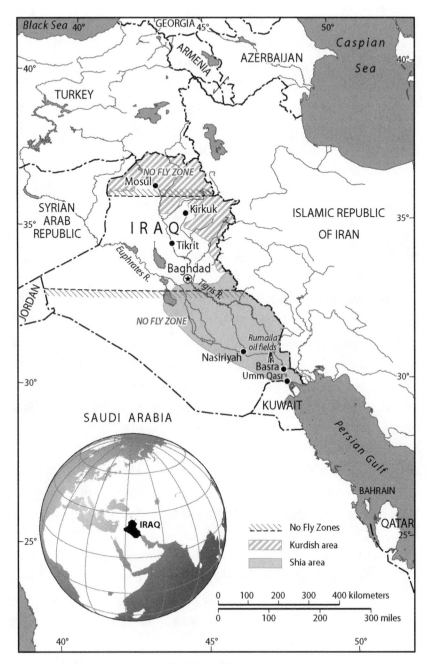

The Iraq Theater

their leaders. It was a moment of enormous significance, a war that had achieved its stated objectives quickly and relatively painlessly. War worked, it seemed, at least against Iraq. Moreover, it worked politically at home. The clean, clear-cut victory returned Americans to the basics—to life, to sacrifice, to honor, and to victory abroad. Even the bitter aftertaste of Vietnam receded. The president's approval rating briefly soared to 91 percent.

Even as the war was ending, however, some Americans had begun to see that we had set our sights too low. If Saddam Hussein was so bad, why stop with liberating Kuwait? Among the American leaders calling for action to remove Saddam Hussein from power was President Bush himself, who suggested that the people of Iraq overthrow him. The common expectation in Washington was that his defeat would, one way or the other, result in Saddam's loss of power in Iraq.

Inside Iraq, the aftermath of the war was complicated. Incited by the United States and its victory over Saddam, Shiite Muslims in the south, long sympathetic to neighboring Iran, and the Kurdish minority in the north began rebellions that threatened Saddam's rule. The insurrections were brutally repressed by Saddam, and the U.S. failed to intercede. In the north Saddam's campaign against the Kurds was blocked by the imposition of an Iraqi no-fly zone, a humanitarian relief mission, and threats of U.S. intervention should Saddam attempt to repress the Kurdish elements there.

What followed was an angry cessation of hostilities, with Iraq sanctioned by the UN until the complete dismantlement of its mass destruction weapons could be verified, and with various quarrels along the border with Kuwait about specific boundary demarcation.

Over the next nine years Iraq remained a vexing problem for

the United States: Unable to verify that Iraq had fully given up its weapons of mass destruction, the United States insisted on UN inspections, sanctions, and, beginning in late 1998, a nearly continuous bombing campaign—with hundreds of strikes over more than four years—as U.S. and British aircraft trolled the no-fly zones. At the same time, the United States strengthened its military presence in the Persian Gulf and built up capabilities in Kuwait to enable it to refight the war—only bigger, better, and faster. And Saddam Hussein remained the archetypal Middle East villain—and a particular enemy of Israel.

Step by step in 1991 and 1992, the United States established a postwar security presence in Kuwait itself, creating an equipment storage depot at Camp Doha, building up a headquarters staff and periodically redeploying troops for purposes of deterring Iraqi pressures against a Kuwait struggling to regain a sense of security. Even the new administration under Bill Clinton couldn't quite escape the Iraq problem. In 1993 the Iraqis plotted to assassinate the former president, George H. W. Bush, during his visit to Kuwait. The United States responded by launching a cruise missile strike against Iraq's intelligence headquarters. It was a demonstration of U.S. power to the region—and a reminder to Saddam of American hostility. Saddam waited a year and then, in reprise, sent his best divisions south toward Kuwait, where they reoccupied some of the same assembly areas they had used in 1990 to stage the invasion of Kuwait. The United States immediately deployed aircraft and alerted U.S. troops for deployment. If it was only an Iraqi feint, it nevertheless generated a renewed American determination not to be caught off-guard again.

Meanwhile, the UN Special Commission in Iraq (UNSCOM) continued its efforts to verify Iraq's compliance with its pledge to give up weapons of mass destruction. The inspections apparently impacted on the Iraqi program, despite Iraqi denial and deception. And according to Saddam's defecting son-in-law, most of the Iraqi chemical, biological, and nuclear weapons programs were dismantled in the early 1990s. But Iraq remained defiant toward the UN and the United States.

Beyond the UN sanctions, the United States kept the pressure on Saddam's regime according to its Persian Gulf policy of "dual containment": For example, U.S. air forces stationed in Saudi Arabia and Turkey regularly flew over the southern and northern no-fly zones imposed in the aftermath of the war; and the U.S. military presence in the region was strengthened.

Indeed, the threat from Iraq came to assume a major role in U.S. defense planning. A refight of Desert Storm was one of only two scenarios that could be publicly cited to justify large military forces. The other was a North Korean attack across the Demilitarized Zone into the South. By the late 1990s the Persian Gulf had been designated for planning purposes as one of two Major Theaters of War, and systematic investments were undertaken to strengthen logistics, communications, and intelligence in preparation for possible conflict there. In addition, scenarios from hypothetical war in Iraq were used in requirements studies for weapons procurements, force designs, and training.

Meanwhile, Iraq's intransigence with the UN inspectors fed U.S. concerns. One of the principal concerns of the Clinton administration had been proliferation of weapons of mass destruction—and Saddam was consistently defying the UN and U.S. efforts to force inspections and end his programs. When Iraq ended all cooperation with the UN inspectors in the autumn of 1998, stronger measures were required. The U.S. Congress passed the Iraq Liberation Act, calling for regime change in Iraq.

By mid-December 1998, facing continued Iraqi defiance of the UN inspection effort, the United States used force. Operation Desert Fox was launched by U.S. Central Command on December 15 and, over a period of eighty-four hours, pummeled Iraqi headquarters and suspected production and storage sites for weapons of mass destruction.

Saddam struck back, attempting to assert his power by challenging the UN-imposed no-fly zones with brief, in-and-out flights by MiG23 and 25 interceptors flying so fast that the coalition air forces were unable to actually interdict the flights. In retaliation the United States changed its rules of engagement for strikes within the no-fly zones. Beginning in late December 1998, U.S. and British aircraft enforcing the southern and northern no-fly zones engaged any radar or associated facilities that might threaten their aircraft.

As the November 2000 presidential election approached, many within the Republican Party cited Iraq as dangerous unfinished business—a code word for weak leadership by the Democratic president.

Work on a new policy for Iraq began soon after the inauguration of the new president, George W. Bush, when Secretary of State Colin Powell visited the region in February 2001. He returned a few days later to call for narrower, more focused sanctions—the so-called smart sanctions—as a way of rebuilding UN support for the sanctions regime. But the effort died inside the Bush administration itself, as a crisis with China stemming from its detention of a U.S. reconnaissance plane, and later the administration's pursuit of a U.S. national missile defense system, seemed to take center stage.

The terrorist strikes of September 11, 2001, on the World Trade Center and the Pentagon marked a turning point—for the administration, for the United States, and for U.S. relations with the world. It was a cataclysmic event, as forces threatening us from abroad had shattered our sense of security and image of invulnerability here at home. Nothing would ever be the same. It was as if somehow no other state, anywhere, had ever experienced terror. Of course, the scale of loss was utterly devastating—but other nations had lived with fear and the prospect of sudden, surprising deaths, and they had survived. Germany had its Baader-Meinhof gang, Italy the Red Brigades, Britain the Irish Republican Army, Spain the Basque separatists, Greece November 17th, Turkey the PKK. Saudi Arabia, Egypt, India, and of course Israel—all had experienced terrorism. The United States had been struck, of course, in 1993, when explosives planted in the World Trade Center shocked Manhattan the first time. Yet the term "terrorism" had hardly penetrated the American psyche.

But the 9/11 strikes were different, totally different. Massive in scale, monstrous in motive and portentous of horror to come. September 11 was a "discontinuity"—beyond the range of our experience—and it demanded a response. It therefore became an opportunity—an opportunity to lead, an opportunity to build, an opportunity to heal, an opportunity to strike back, an opportunity to reorder the priorities.

President Bush "gripped" the problem, rallying the nation, confronting the fearful, and leading the administration to craft a powerful and effective response to the attacks. The deaths, the trauma, and the fear of repeated attacks provided the leverage to reshape U.S. policy and public perceptions.

Even on the day of 9/11—as Osama bin Laden was becoming a household name in America—there were suggestions from some quarters to seek "state sponsorship" and to name Saddam Hussein as the real culprit behind the terrorists. Hostile, aggressive, stymied—but still striving to pursue his grand transformation of the region—Saddam was unfinished business, a rogue leader who had defied the international community and had made no secret of his support for various anti-Israeli terrorists over the years. Some kind of connection to the perpetrators of 9/11 certainly sounded plausible, and at the minimum Saddam posed a continuing challenge to the U.S.

Although the administration did not at the time conclusively establish Saddam's complicity, over the next eighteen months looming conflict with Iraq came to dominate the war against terror. Arguments and evidence would be presented; the case taken to Congress, the U.S. and the American people. And ultimately the U.S. would act. Whether this was wise policy is a matter to be dealt with later. But it was a reflection of strong and determined leadership, using the most reliable and effective instrument of the U.S. government: its armed forces.

Usually, militaries fight wars they haven't prepared for. This one would be different. General plans had been in place for a decade, backed up by substantial preparations. And from this base, detailed planning began in January 2002, with the first in a series of planning meetings between General Tommy Franks, who was the theater commander, and Secretary of Defense Donald Rumsfeld. The existing plans at U.S. Central Command, OPLAN 1003, had generally followed the Gulf War model of large forces and an extended air campaign at the outset. These were the principle issues that were hammered at during the next fourteen months, with Franks and U.S. Army officials arguing for stronger ground forces, the Secretary of Defense seeking smaller ground forces and a faster-paced campaign. Apparently OPLAN 1003 went through some twenty revisions. The president himself received at least a dozen detailed briefings on the evolving plan.[1]

This incessant back-and-forth made sense. Any standing plan, such as OPLAN 1003 series, would necessarily have been both overly general and risk-averse. Many in each of the armed services could have objected to one or more aspects of the on-the-shelf plan, for it would have reflected a high degree of compromise among the services and commands that were participating in the planning—all made in the absence of specific strategic, diplomatic, and political objectives. Challenging this military planning was fully within the authority of the Secretary of Defense and the President—and given a challenge, many of the assumptions and compromises of the plan were probably unsupportable. The plan could be adjusted and sharpened to suit their immediate concerns.

The challenges served other purposes, too. First, they helped educate and prepare the civilian advisers and the defense secretary himself for the conduct of the operation. The continuing give-and-take ground down the inherent professional experience–based authority of the military leaders and transferred the insights to the civilian interrogators. "Why couldn't it be done thus and so?" "Can you prove that it takes this much or that kind of force?" "What's the basis for such an assumption?" And as the military authorities jockeyed and parried, trying to demonstrate their knowledge and assert their skills while simultaneously strengthening relationships and gaining stature with the secretary, they would expose their internal differences: They could be shaped, played off against each other, and most importantly, their power and control would flow upward—to the civilians. It was a natural process, one that good civilian leaders quickly mastered, because it was the essence of "civilian control."

The continued struggle over the plan resulted in a series of leaks to the press, disclosing much of the concept long before the plan was executed. For example, it was clear that the planners saw Baghdad as the enemy's center of gravity, and its occupation as the key to success. In order to achieve this they would need to defeat the enemy's ground forces, especially the Republican Guards, which in turn would likely require the destruction of the enemy's integrated air defense system. And both of those objectives could be furthered if the Iraqi command and control system—the network of radars, observation posts, command centers, and headquarters—could be destroyed. And because that network was highly centralized around Saddam himself, destruction of the regime—so-called regime targets—became the means as well as the end.

The planners had to consider possible Iraqi countermoves and how to block them. Among such countermoves would have been missile strikes against the coalition staging areas in Kuwait; mining coastal waters and attacking coalition naval forces in the Persian Gulf; chemical weapons strikes against coalition forces concentrating near Baghdad; striking Israel with SCUD missiles and weapons of mass destruction; and the suicidal and environmentally catastrophic destruction of Iraq's oil fields to poison the hopes of any occupation.

What emerged was an integrated plan built around three components: A strong air offensive would go after regime targets and destroy Iraq's integrated air defense system; special operating forces would conduct strikes to take out SCUD launching facilities in western Iraq and defeat any Iraqi naval capabilities near Umm Qasr; and ground forces would move into Baghdad as quickly as possible, defeating any remaining Iraqi forces en route. Each part would reinforce the others. Special forces would tie down Iraqi freedom of maneuver, call in air strikes, and provide deep reconnaissance for ground forces. The air offensive would destroy Iraqi command and control and air defenses and then concentrate on destroying enemy ground forces. And coalition ground forces would force the Iraqis to maneuver and expose themselves to attack from the air. Ideally, all three elements operating together would move so quickly that no effective and in-depth defense of Baghdad would be prepared.

These elements were reinforced by efforts to impede Iraqi preparations through misinformation, deception, and psychological operations using the news media, journalists, former Iraqi generals, and direct communications, including e-mail with Iraqi leaders. The intent was to persuade Iraqis to lay down their arms, to refrain from using chemical and biological weapons even if ordered to do so, and to defect. This was the so-called information war. It had become a major growth industry inside the military since the 1991 war in the Gulf; it promised success more cheaply, with fewer casualties, by using modern technology and exploiting so-called asymmetric U.S. advantages. Interestingly, though, some of the ideas and concepts—like sowing fear and confusion among the enemy—were anything but novel.

Some of these activities had begun even while the UN inspections were still under way. Teams of paramilitary operatives under the U.S. Central Intelligence Agency (CIA) were inserted into Iraq, where they made contact with dissident groups and even had contact with some prominent military officials and Baath leaders. Leaflet drops began long before the anticipated beginning of the military action. And there were preparations to use the full technical capabilities of U.S. forces, including the ability to take over radio frequencies and intrude over the Internet.

In addition, the plan would take advantage of the ongoing air strikes into the northern and southern no-fly zones in an effort to prepare the battlefield by ripping apart Iraqi air defenses, communications, command and control, and long-range artillery and missiles commencing in mid-2002.

As war plans and planning processes go, this had to be one of the most detailed and meticulous ever conducted. The plan to invade Normandy was finalized in just four months—after General Dwight D. Eisenhower, the supreme Allied commander, arrived at a new headquarters fresh from the campaign in Sicily in early 1944. The war in Korea was fought with defensive plans on the fly, and General Douglas MacArthur launched the Inchon invasion with less than ninety days of planning and preparation. In the 1991 Gulf War, the planning consumed some five months. In Kosovo in 1999, the planning for the ground campaign wasn't even permitted until the air campaign had been under way for the better part of a month. But the proof of the plan would not be in its elegant formulation but in its execution—it must provide resources and a framework for mastering the unexpected.

As the planning moved forward, though, the military plan was only part of the larger diplomatic and strategic considerations associated with turning military success into strategic victory. Here the Bush administration was divided, with some arguing simply to strike, others arguing that at the very least greater international authority should be sought from the UN before going to war. In the late summer of 2002 a decision was made to go to the UN to gain a new Security Council Resolution. We would use U.S. resolve and our overwhelming military power to gain diplomatic leverage.

In early September 2002, the Bush administration took the problem of Iraq to the United Nations. The U.S. intent was never beyond dispute: As framed by the president, it was to deal once and for all with the problem of Iraq's weapons of mass destruction. But to others, the intent seemed more to gain UN approval for a war that the United States was determined to wage regardless. The gauntlet was thrown down, as the president challenged the UN to act—or the United States would. After all, it wasn't as though the United States really needed the UN's support—at least not in any military sense. This wasn't a helpless Haile Selassie of Ethiopia making a last desperate appeal to the League of Nations as foreign invaders were ripping through his country. No, this was the world's lone superpower requesting, demanding, challenging: Act—or we will. Driven by overwhelming U.S. power, and strong U.S. and British leadership, the UN succeeded in producing a resolution on Iraq that would have been impossible a year or two earlier. It seemed also to prove one of the continuing ironies of diplomacy: The threat to act alone is sometimes the best means to encourage action together.

Unanimously passed, Security Council Resolution 1441 set a series of timelines by which Saddam Hussein would have to express his intent to comply with the UN resolutions, provide information, and accept renewed and enhanced inspections. The aim was to prescribe clear, unambiguous standards with which Iraq must quickly comply, and to which the international community could hold Iraq accountable.

However, the language was in fact a compromise. On the one hand, it met European and Russian concerns, calling for the United States to consult with the UN before taking action in the event that Saddam failed to comply. On the other, the wording was such that the United States could claim authority to go to war without a second resolution. As John Negroponte, the U.S. ambassador to the UN, explained, "If the Security Council fails to act decisively in the event of further Iraqi violation, this resolution does not constrain any member state from acting to defend itself from the threat posed by Iraq or to enforce relevant

United Nations resolutions and protect world peace and security." The key phrase, of course, was "further Iraqi violation," which the resolution would help to develop.

Hence, the victory at the UN was somewhat less than it appeared. It did not reflect a united international position—at least not yet. Many in Europe and elsewhere believed that the United States had already made the decision to go to war. So much of the diplomacy at the UN had been more a last-ditch effort to restrain an American invasion and less a collective effort to solve the problem of Saddam's illegal weaponry. As such, despite the wording of Resolution 1441, further UN support would probably depend on establishing not only the facts of Saddam's failure to comply but also eliminating any other alternative to the use of force, unless Saddam posed an immediate threat.

Moreover, the administration's focus on resolution seemed to preclude initiating postwar planning with the UN. Without international planning and support the United States was depriving itself of on-the-ground and in-the-region legitimacy, and increasing the difficulties of postwar burden-sharing. It was an early indicator of what would become a perplexing administration determination to exclude a meaningful postwar UN role. This failure to seek early support for the postwar mission could later be seen as a serious mistake in U.S. planning and policy.

Europeans' concerns about the administration's actual intent had basis in hard fact, too, for intensive military action against Iraq had already begun. Unknown to the American public, and prior to taking the problem to the UN, the United States decided to expand the air strikes in the southern no-fly zone to destroy Saddam's communications and air defense systems in preparation for the coming war. These strikes were billed as routine retaliation against Saddam's efforts to interfere with coalition flights, but in fact they were the opening stages of "battlefield preparation." They were actually intended to soften up Saddam's defenses to facilitate the later campaign.[2]

Preparations on the ground began in September 2002 when elements of the U.S. 3rd Infantry Division fell in upon the prepositioned sets of equipment located in Kuwait and began desert training. By late November, the theater headquarters elements were shaping up. In a major command-post exercise held in Qatar, component commanders and staffs gathered to work through and refine the war plans. One could argue that the military preparations reinforced the U.S. diplomatic efforts and backed up the UN resolve—but the preparations also seemed to preclude patiently waiting for any diplomatic solution. It was all a matter of perspective.

As the U.S. planning transitioned into actual reserve call-ups and deployments in late autumn, the plans yo-yoed back and forth. Apparently there were quarrels within the Bush administration over the timing and nature of the diplomatic efforts and how they might impact the deployment of forces. As changes to the plan continued, the carefully prepared Time-Phased Force and Deployment Data List—which could take as long as two years to prepare—became another concern. If approved, it would alert, mobilize, and deploy forces in a logical sequence, virtually on autopilot, with each force arriving in priority of employment. It was, Secretary Rumsfeld was reported to have said, "a Cold War relic." He threw it out.

Instead the Secretary of Defense and his closest staff continued to use the Deployment Order, which gave the secretary personal control over each unit and each move. However, appraising each deployment was a time-consuming process for him, and soon word came down that Rumsfeld wanted to approve only "batches" of deployments, built around significant units. These instructions broke the careful sequences that enabled forces to be alerted, mobilized, and readied for deployment in the sequence in which they would be needed. This was especially critical for the reserve forces, many of which had to be augmented with personnel and equipment to meet the theater's requirements. What followed instead was an irregularly timed patchwork process that interspersed early-deploying units with those needed later, delayed mobilization, hampered training, and slowed the overall deployments considerably.

To be sure, the military faced a planning dilemma: Deploying and maintaining large forces prematurely was undesirable—too expensive, too vulnerable, too politically damaging at home, and too disruptive to the diplomatic process and to the region. But delaying the deployments might mean starting without everything in the plan on hand. Perhaps Secretary Rumsfeld felt that only he could, on a day-to-day basis, get the balance right. This gave the secretary the "hands on the dial" control to assure that the military movements were consistent with overarching diplomatic and political considerations. But it also meant that the secretary would have to take the time to examine and approve each of the specific, discrete steps involved in mobilizing and deploying hundreds of active and reserve units for the individual actions. Even for Rumsfeld, a man renowned for his personal energy, this was going to be a stretch. To some within the system, the real motive seemed personal: control. Still, the Secretary's concerns had merit.

In November, the exact start date for the operation was unknowable. Obviously, it would make sense to wait a few weeks if UN support for the attack could be secured. However, if diplomacy were to fail, then the attack would have to follow relatively quickly, before public momentum could disappear. And there was the matter of American public opinion, as well. Polls showed a bare majority of Americans in favor of the attack, but it was assumed that number would grow as conflict appeared more imminent.

There was continuing speculation about difficulties of combat during the approaching hot season, which many read as an attempt by the Pentagon to lock in a date for invasion. This would have imposed a deadline on the operation of mid- to late March 2003. It was a wishful and absurd proposition, as though the soldiers and their equipment would cease functioning once the Iraqi climate reached a specific temperature. Moreover, it ignored both recent experience and common sense. In 1990, the first defensive deployments had occurred in extremely hot weather in Saudi Arabia, with temperatures consistently in the 130-degree range in some locations. At that time the troops remained effective, even though uncomfortable. This time around, what did the Pentagon think would happen afterward, even if the conflict began on schedule? Were the troops suddenly going to depart for the United States before the summer arrived in Iraq? Even Secretary of State Powell remarked that there was no deadline for the operation.

But it made some sense for the Americans to err on the side of being late and light, as the balance of forces in the forthcoming campaign indicated a total mismatch. Defending Iraq, Saddam could nominally call upon twenty-six divisions, comprising perhaps 2,000 tanks, 2,500 pieces of artillery, some 300 fighter and attack aircraft, and maybe 150 armed helicopters. Chemical and biological warfare capabilities had been developed, and at least the chemical weaponry had been employed in the 1980s.

Iraq's forces totaled perhaps 400,000 troops plus as many more reservists, and maybe 40,000 Fedayeen fighters. Of course, Saddam's forces had endured more than a decade of U.S. overflights and air strikes into the northern and southern no-fly zones, plus the intensive air strikes in 1998. They must have had considerable knowledge of the electronic and radar signatures of the coalition forces, their operating patterns, and their procedures. The Iraqis would have studied their own experiences with the Americans in the 1991 Gulf War, as well as receiving information from the Russians, Chinese, and Serbs, all of whom had anxiously monitored the evolution of U.S. forces since the Gulf War.

The Iraqi numbers and experience belied extraordinary weaknesses. Their equipment was old, little changed from the weaponry used against the Iranians in the 1980s; a significant portion could be presumed inoperative. The training for the forces was constrained. And most important, the integrated air defense system was woefully underprepared: Its radars and command centers were vulnerably located, its missiles inadequate in range and speed, its aircraft overmatched, and much of its communications fragile. Without a survivable, effective air defense system, all else would be lost.

Against this aging force the United States matched its best and finest. It had spent most of a decade preparing for this fight. Iraq was ringed with airfields, storage facilities, and friendly governments willing to accommodate U.S. access under the right circumstances. In the air, the fight would be waged by the new B–2 "Spirit" stealth bombers, each carrying up to sixteen 2,000-pound Joint Direct Attack Munitions (JDAM), the inertial- and satellite-guided all-weather bombs that would strike within a few feet of an aim point. The B–2s had first been used in the 1999 Kosovo campaign, where the astonishing accuracy of the

JDAM—falling to a predesignated aim point guided by a constellation of satellites and backed up by an inertial guidance system—proved the key to sustaining a winning, all-weather campaign. The stealth bombers would be supplemented by B–1 bombers. Originally designed during the Cold War to zip below Soviet radar coverage at supersonic speeds to deliver nuclear strikes, B–1s would carry an even heavier load—more than seventy 500-pound bombs or a dozen or more JDAMs. And then there would be the aged but modernized B–52 bombers, launching cruise missiles with 3,000-pound warheads and, when the antiaircraft system was sufficiently degraded, loitering overhead, to provide on-call support. Also, in the early going, there would be the F–117 "Nighthawk" stealth fighters, used against Iraq in the 1991 Gulf War and still effective.

But the improvements to overall U.S. airpower were even broader. First, all U.S. Navy aircraft could now drop precision weapons, and the JDAM could now be dropped by virtually any U.S. combat aircraft. Electronic warfare assets had been strengthened. The EA–6B "Prowler" was augmented with improved self-protection jamming pods carried by other aircraft, and the newer F–16Ds carried antiradiation missiles to home in on enemy radars.

In addition, U.S. forces had spent the preceding decade making their command and control procedures more flexible and responsive. Unmanned aerial vehicles (UAVs) with down-linked full-motion video were able to loiter overhead. Surveillance technology deployed in space, as well as the high-flying U–2 spy planes, had been improved. Increased numbers of improved Joint Surveillance and Target Acquisition Radar Systems (JSTARS) were acquired and integrated more closely into the air strike planning system. There was a sustained effort to strengthen the sensor-to-shooter linkages between the reconnaissance assets and the strike elements. And the system had been refined in action in Afghanistan in 2001, in Kosovo in 1999, in earlier strikes against Iraq in 1998, and in strikes in Bosnia in 1995.

U.S. ground forces were also at high readiness. New nighttime sights, new communications, new trucks, and a far richer deployment of navigation equipment, as well as a leadership honed by nearly continuous deployments for training and peace operations, enabled a new, more intense style of U.S. warfare. In addition, the U.S. 3rd Infantry Division had spent months in the desert training and honing their live-fire skills. In the crucial direct-fire battles to come, the U.S. forces aimed to have every advantage. They had also used the time to refine their procedures to bring in artillery and air support. Thus, for all its reduction in numbers, this was a force far more capable, on a unit-for-unit basis, than the larger force that fought the Gulf War in 1991.

Major deployment uncertainties revolved around support (or nonsupport) from two allies: Turkey and Saudi Arabia. The stakes were high. Turkey's support would enable deployment of forces through eastern Turkey to attack southward into Iraq, shut down the possibility of a separate Kurdish state, quickly gain control of the oil fields around Kirkuk, and enable forces to attack Baghdad and Tikrit, Saddam's main area of support, from the north. The use of Saudi ports would enable a much larger per-day throughput of forces and supplies and therefore give the force more flexibility in reacting to the constraints and unpredictabilities of diplomacy or threats against Kuwait. And the use of Saudi airspace would greatly facilitate air and special operations throughout western Iraq especially. Both allies were important; neither was absolutely essential.

In the case of Turkey, the election of a new government, headed by Recep Erdogan, the turnover of its top military leadership in the autumn of 2002, and the country's long, tiring campaign to gain entry into the European Union (EU) made it more difficult to obtain its support. Negotiations were held under the auspices of the U.S. embassy in Ankara but ultimately collapsed amid Turkish concerns about lack of UN support, EU pressures, Turkish skepticism of U.S. resolve, and domestic politics.

Not until a few days into the war would Turkey approve the use of Turkish airspace for overflight, and it would continue to deny U.S. ground troops permission to deploy. The result was that a major part of the planned U.S. force, the ultramodern U.S. 4th Infantry Division (Mechanized), was becalmed in ships in the Mediterranean Sea off the coast of Turkey from mid-February until early April.

The Saudis, meanwhile, were working to balance their domestic resistance to the war and to an increased U.S. presence with their long-standing commitments to support U.S. aims in the region. After some conflicting statements during the final diplomatic efforts in January and early February, Saudi support stabilized around a formula that gave the United States permission to use the airspace and headquarters but not to use the ports or deploy major ground forces through Saudi Arabia. There were reports of special forces deploying and staging in Saudi Arabia, however.

The ultimate result was that U.S. ground forces were constrained to deploy through Kuwait City, which could accommodate some three to six ships per day—equipment for perhaps 15–20 percent of a single U.S. Army division—and an average of about twenty-four wide-bodied aircraft per day. The United States had taken the precaution of prepositioning considerable equipment in or near the area—a U.S. Army brigade set in Kuwait another additional brigades afloat, plus in Qatar, a third prepositioning for a Marine expeditionary brigade—but if the equipment and supplies had to be offloaded in Kuwait, these port facilities presented the same problem as deployment from the continental United States or Europe. This constraint was compounded by the additional tonnage required to support forward deployments of combat aircraft.

By late December 2002 the planning had come down to a race to complete essential deployments before the diplomacy concluded—without, at the same time, deploying so much that the diplomacy was fatally compromised.

As for the diplomatic front, Saddam failed to submit new details in December 2002 corroborating his stated compliance with the UN Security Council resolutions. It seemed that Saddam was in a deep dilemma: Either he "toughed it out," denying the existence of any weapons programs and daring the United States to act, or he submitted details that proved his earlier duplicity. In this case, he was hanging tough. But this assumed that there was something to conceal—and that was the essence of the dispute. Still, Saddam lived up to his reputation by continuing to prickle and resist at the margins. Iraqi acceptance of the enhanced inspections remained grudging at best. There were contending views as to the next steps, with some nations proposing more extensive inspections and additional reporting. But for the Bush administration, the outcome was assured: Saddam was in violation, and military force could be used as provided in UN Security Council Resolution 1441.

Faced with British prime minister Tony Blair's need for legitimacy and diplomatic cover, the United States and UK returned to the UN in January 2003 to seek a "second resolution" in the

Security Council. But the deep divisions that strong U.S. pressure and British diplomacy had papered over in the autumn were no longer manageable. The diplomacy stuttered, stalled, and ultimately failed. There would be no second Security Council resolution, and there would be no UN plan for postwar reconstruction and governance. The United States would be on its own, assisted by the UK and some token contributions from Australia.

For some in the Bush administration, the UN's failure to authorize action against Saddam was entirely predictable. They saw the UN as feckless, hobbled by conflicting aims, and committed to appeasing rather than resolving threats to peace and security. This, they claimed, was exactly the failure the president had warned against in his September 2002 address to the UN.

But for many foreign officials—in Europe and elsewhere—the perceptions were different. They questioned the sufficiency of the evidence and the need to go to war when the inspections hadn't been concluded and seemed to be achieving more than ever before. There were also larger concerns about an American hyperpower that was so powerful it could break treaties and deny international obligations with impunity. This was a fear that the administration itself had abetted soon after taking office, when it walked out on the Kyoto Treaty, worked against the International Criminal Court, and threatened to withdraw from the Anti-Ballistic Missile Treaty. Long-standing disagreement between the United States and its European allies over how to resolve the continuing conflict between Israel and the Palestinians also complicated the achievement of anything like consensus on the issues at hand.

Focused on commencing the operations, the United States forfeited another opportunity to salvage international legitimacy and assistance in the immediate postwar tasks. It was an oversight that reflected the unilateralist approach that critics abroad cited as stereotypical and that had caused the United States to lose so much of the international sympathy and support it received after 9/11. It would also cost American soldiers, the administration, and taxpayers dearly in the aftermath.

By March 17, 2003, the final diplomatic efforts had collapsed. President Bush then gave Saddam Hussein a forty-eight-hour deadline to leave Iraq.

The diplomatic collapse caught the U.S. military preparations in midstride. The air and naval forces were largely in position—only two of the five aircraft carriers planned for the operation had failed to close, and these would be able to launch their aircraft across Saudi and Turkish airspace—but much of the planned U.S. ground force wasn't ready. The 101st Airborne Division was still unloading and staging its final two brigades through the airfield and port in Kuwait. Helicopters remained to be assembled, and the force needed to move to its assembly areas and begin final preparations. The 4th Infantry Division's equipment was still packed aboard ships in the Mediterranean, while most of its troops remained at Fort Hood, Texas. The 1st Armored Division, based in Germany, hadn't begun its deployment. The 1st Cavalry Division, also alerted for deployment, was still in Fort Hood. Additional commands such as the 3rd Armored Cavalry Regiment from Fort Carson, Colorado, and the 2nd Light Cavalry Regiment from Fort Polk, Louisiana, also remained Stateside.

This left the coalition with only three division-sized forces plus two separate brigades fully ready at the opening of the campaign: the U.S. 3rd Infantry Division, which had completed its full deployment in January; the U.S. Marine Expeditionary

Force, whose ground component consisted of the U.S. 1st Marine Division from Camp Pendleton, California; the scaled-down British 1st Armored Division, pulled from forces in the UK and Germany; and 2nd Brigade, 82nd Airborne, and the Marines Task Force Tarawa. And all were located in Kuwait—no force was located to the north in Turkey.

As for air operations, the moonlight data were somewhat unfavorable. The full moon—100 percent illumination—would occur the next night, March 18. Doctrinally, U.S. air planners would prefer to use the new moon periods, when the skies are darkest, to initiate air strikes against an operational air defense system. While probably not essential, the darkness simply provides one additional means of protection for the aircraft, some of which might be seen in the moonlight even at high altitudes.

Still, the less-than-optimal circumstances could be used to best advantage to create surprise. Even the Turks considered it unlikely that the United States would follow through with an attack unless the U.S. 4th Infantry Division was deployed into northern Iraq through Turkey. And Saddam left up to seven divisions deployed north of Baghdad, which may well have indicated his belief that the real threat would come from the north.[3]

In fact, the operation was largely ready to go. It would open with a forty-eight-hour window for special operations to begin deep reconnaissance and direct-action missions inside Iraq. U.S. Special Operations Forces (SOF) would join the previously deployed CIA teams to attack communications, call in air strikes, and provide on-the-ground reporting for the air and ground forces to follow. Thirty-one teams, some 300 people, entered Iraq during the hours of darkness on the night of March 19–20. The air operation was then planned to begin on Friday, March 21. A brief window of total darkness, right after sunset, would be followed about two hours later by almost full moonlight for the rest of the night.

The unanticipated intelligence that located Saddam and his sons, Uday and Qusay, south of Baghdad precluded the planned start. Instead of the shock and awe of several thousand warheads and missiles, two F–117s were launched early, striking at dawn on March 20. Operation Iraqi Freedom had formally begun.

During the hours of darkness and into the early morning of March 20, the U.S. Army, Marines, and British forces moved from their assembly areas to attack positions, from where they would stage and prepare to cross the Kuwaiti border. The plan called for the Army forces to move west initially, then northwest into the desert, skirting the populated Euphrates Valley as they angled toward the Karbala Gap southwest of Baghdad. The Marines would initially move to secure the Rumaila oil fields, then turn northwest and north, eventually moving into the fertile valley between the Euphrates and Tigris Rivers and closing on Baghdad from the south. The British forces would focus initially on southern Iraq, centering their efforts around Basra, then moving north to protect the U.S. Marines' right flank as forces became available.

One key issue during the planning had been how soon to commence the ground phase. Clearly, timing would depend on battlefield results, trade-offs, and risks. Commanders would want the ground forces to move as soon as they could be assured of air support when they needed it, then close in around Baghdad, for the sooner the force moved to and penetrated Baghdad, the lower the risk of facing a well-coordinated urban defense in the capital. At the beginning of the planning process, as much as two weeks had been allowed for the air operation before the ground troops would advance. By January, the time had been whittled down to

as little as a four-day air operation.[4] But in the days preceding the
beginning of the air attack, it had become increasingly clear that
the Iraqi air defense and ground forces were not going to be a significant challenge except in the Baghdad area.

The preference was to move in the ground force early and
sustain its forward momentum. This made military sense and
was also in keeping with the overriding political concerns to
fight and finish quickly. But the trigger events may have been
reports that the Iraqis were beginning to destroy the Rumaila oil
field, a key U.S. objective, and the Iraqi missile response to the
U.S. attack on Saddam Hussein. At least four missiles were fired
into Kuwait. Two were the CSS–3 Silkworms, the big Chinese
surface-to-surface missiles intended originally to strike naval
vessels. The others were ballistic, including the Ababil–100, an
unguided, solid-fuel missile with a range of a little more than
100 miles (in violation, by the way, of UN restrictions). They
were capable of carrying chemical and biological weapons, as
well as high explosives. At least three missiles were shot down by
U.S.-made Patriot antimissile missiles.

The missiles had clearly been targeted against U.S. forces.
Somehow, the Iraqis had received intelligence on the locations
of the U.S. assembly areas. The first missile was launched Thursday, March 20, at "Thunder Road," the assembly area for the
101st Airborne Division. An hour later another missile was
launched against Camp Doha, the headquarters for the coalition
land forces. Another missile went after the rear staging area at
Camp Udari.

And so the coalition response was logical: Move early, secure
the oil fields, overrun the missile launching sites, get out of the
target zone of the missiles, and take advantage of the start of the
air campaign and the possible destruction of Iraq's senior lead-

ership. The ground attack, planned to begin on Saturday morning, was advanced twenty-four hours.

Army and Marine forces opened their attacks with artillery and rocket barrages, followed by a wave of Cobra attack helicopters in front of the Marines, peppering suspected or reported enemy positions. Engineers moved first, marking routes through the berms, antitank ditches, and minefields surrounding Kuwait. Scattered contact with enemy forces was reported.

About the same time, a second round of cruise missile and aircraft strikes was directed against enemy command centers, air defense, and regime targets in and around Baghdad, as well as in the north near Mosul.

In western Iraq, Special Operations Forces were taking action, directed at Iraqi airfields and facilities believed to be associated with Iraq's intent to strike Israel. They were based in Jordan and Saudi Arabia, apparently, and would eventually total some 10,000 Army, Navy, and Air Force personnel.

For the United States, the first twenty-four hours were auspicious: an intelligence windfall, an agile decapitating strike aimed at Saddam Hussein, special operations under way, several near-misses by enemy rockets and missiles in Kuwait, no friendly losses, and U.S. and British forces on the move. As the sun rose on the morning of Friday, March 21, television viewers around the world were treated to the incredible spectacle of one of the lead armored cavalry troops of the U.S. 3rd Infantry Division flashing across an open desert at breakneck speeds. This war was now for real, and there was euphoria in the air—at least in the United States. President Bush was lucky, so very lucky, it was said. But could he really have already won this war by knocking off Saddam Hussein with the first blow?

CHAPTER 2

ROLLING NORTH

A FEW HOURS after the decapitating U.S. strike, Iraqi TV broadcast a TV taped message from Saddam Hussein. He spoke of Iraq's inevitable victory over the Americans. At the time, news media took the tape with skepticism; was the image really Saddam? Wasn't the United States operating off good intelligence, and if so, then how could Saddam have escaped? And when, in a subsequent broadcast, he praised the commander of a force that had already surrendered, well, wasn't it likely that these appearances had been prepared in advance?

Later it was discovered that the commander hadn't surrendered after all; he and most of the division had simply taken off their uniforms and faded back into Basra to continue to fight—the man who had supposedly surrendered the division wasn't its commander at all, just an imposter. And apparently Saddam had not been killed in the strike. No, victory would not come quite so easily.

At daybreak on March 21, the U.S. Army's 3rd Infantry Division, consisting of about 20,000 troops and almost 10,000 vehicles, continued to move, flowing from assembly areas in Kuwait, moving across the berm, and striking into the Iraqi desert. The 20,000 Marines moved generally to the northeast, where their objective was to seize the Rumaila oil fields to prevent their destruction, secure the main route, Route 8, through Safwan to Basra, and clean up local Iraqi forces. The British were moving overland and by helicopter to reinforce the special forces in the vicinity of Basra and points south.

On the Fao Peninsula, a combined U.S.-British special forces operation was launched against Iraqi naval and petroleum facilities. The intent was to prevent any Iraqi naval operation that might interfere with coalition naval activities, either by releasing mines or dumping crude oil into the Persian Gulf. By daybreak a combined U.S.-British Marine operation saw 4,000 British Royal Marines from the 3rd Commando Brigade seize key Iraqi facilities. They were joined a few hours later by the U.S. 15th Marine Expeditionary Unit, a battalion-sized force that launched from the Persian Gulf to seize control of key facilities in the port city of Umm Qasr.

Over the next seventy-two hours, the lead elements of the 3rd Infantry Division penetrated about 250 miles into Iraq, clearing a wide swath of desert for follow-on forces, seizing the Talil airfield, grabbing a bridge over the Euphrates River, and bypassing the towns along the way. The intent was to bypass populated areas, not to contest them. Focus on the enemy forces; get to Baghdad, the enemy's "center of gravity." Above all, move quickly and move deep.

Truck-mounted troops of the 101st Airborne (Air Assault) moved into Iraq, following the same route blazed by the 3rd Infantry Division. Forces from the U.S. 1st Marine Division moved to the north and east from Kuwait, seizing much of the

Rumaila oil fields. In western Iraq, special forces seized key terrain overlooking the H–2 and H–3 air bases, in a successful bid to preclude their use to support SCUD launches against Israel. And in northern Iraq, special forces operating with the Kurds captured an air base.

"Shock and awe," the preplanned air campaign, kicked in on the evening of March 21. Three waves of strikes delivered more than 1,300 bombs and missiles targeted at command and control systems, communications, air defenses, and units of the Republican Guards and Special Republican Guards. Many of the strikes were targeted at or around Baghdad, but other facilities in northern and western Iraq were also struck. One set of strikes included some 320 Tomahawk cruise missiles, B–1 and B–2 bombers and the whole range of strike aircraft. Targets were planned to minimize the chances of accidental civilian casualties. In addition, A–10 close support attack planes, AC–130 gunships, and F/A–18 fighter-bombers supported the advance of the ground forces and struck Iraqi facilities in southern Iraq. Most of the action was American, with some assistance from UK strike aircraft and submarine-launched ballistic missiles. Army long-range missiles were also used.

These were the strikes that had dominated the thinking of the U.S. Air Force for decades. Strike hard initially, the theory went, and take out the enemy's command and control systems, air defenses, and ability to repair. Take it down all at once, before the enemy could anticipate the real power of the strikes or harden himself and his public opinion to withstand them. It reflected the pride of an independent Air Force, no longer chained to the plodding pace of the "ground-pounders." It was the legacy of the big B–52 strikes in late 1972 against Hanoi, when we broke the power of North Vietnamese air defenses and brought Vietnamese leaders to the negotiating table for real. The Big Win strategy had been attempted in the Gulf War, going "downtown" with the air power all the way to Baghdad, and was refined since with new equipment and tactics.

In the Kosovo campaign, the big strikes remained the airmen's ideal, the theoretical way to win—a single, sustained knockout blow that would decimate an adversary's will to resist. "Turn out the lights in Belgrade" my air commanders asserted, again and again. And even after success in Kosovo, some airmen remained unsatisfied, even angry, that leaders in the North Atlantic Treaty Organization (NATO) had denied them the right to try out their theory of how to win. They were so confident. In Afghanistan, the thinking went, there weren't enough so-called high-value targets to make a difference.

But now, against Iraq, here was the opportunity to prove the theory, provided the intelligence was good and the theater commander, General Tommy Franks, and the secretary of defense weren't too timid in risking civilian casualties. But as always, some targets were withheld, either to reduce unnecessary damage to the civilian infrastructure that would be needed after the war, or to maintain the continuing surrender talks with Iraqi commanders. The strikes were tough, but they were not unrestricted. And the airpower theory would remain, once more, unproven.

The personal air campaign against Saddam Hussein also continued. By Friday evening reports suggested he had moved north to his Tharthar compound near Tikrit. Soon coalition forces pounded it in a volley of cruise missiles, reportedly collapsing both ends of the building.

During the first few days Iraqi resistance throughout the country was light: a few more missiles fired at Kuwait; several armored vehicles at or near the border engaged and destroyed;

some artillery fire in the vicinity of Basra and Umm Qasr; two Marines killed in a firefight; coordinated antiaircraft fire over Baghdad (but less fearsome than that experienced twelve years before during the Gulf War). The chief coalition concern seemed to be the nonbattle losses. First, a U.S. helicopter carrying eight British Royal Marines had crashed, then two British helicopters had collided; in both cases, all on board died.

The coalition was building strong momentum with its advance, but progress on the ground was not matched by the surrender of large numbers of Iraqi soldiers. Most were just melting away in civilian clothes, some to continue the fight. And though there were no signs of chemical or biological weapons, the attitude of the Iraqi civilians was problematic. Where were the joyous demonstrations? Where were the spontaneous uprisings to support the Americans—something promised by the Iraqi exiles—that would have been so useful in shaping world opinion and solidifying domestic support in the United States and UK? The populous seemed ambivalent, hesitant to show support for the Americans and Brits.

The United States pressed hard on the information. Under U.S. guidance, former Iraqi generals contacted the Iraqi military leadership. E-mail attacks continued, and radio frequencies were used to broadcast coalition messages. "Don't resist. Don't use chemical weapons. Surrender your forces." Worldwide TV coverage of the advancing American troops, available to be viewed in Baghdad, was part of the big message, too—so disturbing to the regime that the Iraqi Ministry of Information forced the CNN crew in Baghdad to leave the country.

Meanwhile Iraqi officials were waging their own information campaign, escorting TV reporters around Baghdad to point out the alleged mistakes of the bombing campaign. Many non-U.S.

television networks were broadcasting images of hapless women and children reported to be victims of the bombing.

This was modern war: The media was part of the campaign itself. And governments knew it. Small tactical actions, mistakes and accidents, and civilian casualties can almost instantly exert major influence on domestic and international opinion. Public opinion itself becomes a weapon of war, able to be aroused and manipulated with rapid effect on the campaign itself. It was the American media, rooting for their troops against an evil dictator, against the relatively new Arab media, led by Al Jazeera, portraying the horror of war and the aggressiveness of the Americans. For the media, this was about truth as they saw it—through their own culture, experience, and environment. And the truth was, like it or not, relative.

But the United States had taken the surest approach to minimize the effectiveness of Iraqi information operations: It had "embedded" more than 500 members of the media, including at least one reporter from Al Jazeera, into the U.S. air, land, and sea forces. Despite some initial concerns about operational security, the embedding program was proving to be a great success. Reporters were able to show the human face of the U.S. forces, along with unprecedented real-time access to the uncertainties, fears, and hardships of the ground battle. It was, intentionally or not, a program that won great sympathy for the American forces in the field, at least among the public back home. The earnestness and candor of the soldiers cemented the already rising public support for the American effort.

Ironically, even the exposure of incidents the military would not have liked shown—for example scenes of a U.S. soldier who attacked an officers' sleeping tent of 1st Brigade, 101st Airborne—provided a realism and drama that enhanced the credibility of the media and the forces themselves.

In addition, the United States was taking strong and necessary precautions—procedures perfected during previous campaigns—to minimize civilian casualties, especially as a result of air actions. The smallest bombs and missiles were selected so that targets would be hit with the barest minimum power necessary to destroy them. In some cases the aim points of strikes were reportedly "offset" from the centers of the targets to reduce damage to nearby structures. Suspected chemical and biological weapons storage facilities were avoided, as were "dual-use" targets like electric power facilities.

Despite concerns that such restrictions might vitiate the effectiveness of the air strikes, the air operation maintained a high intensity on Saturday and overnight into Sunday. U.S. aircraft continued to target Iraqi command and control and other regime targets in Baghdad with as many as 500 strikes, as well as in the north around Mosul.

By nightfall on Sunday, March 23, the 3rd Infantry Division's lead elements had bypassed the town of Najaf and reached within 100 miles of the capital, and it was here that they encountered the first organized Iraqi resistance. Consisting of a few tanks, antiaircraft guns, and irregular infantry dug into the desert behind sandbags along the crest of an escarpment, and reinforced by a few tubes of artillery, this force provided a "security zone" position in front of the anticipated Iraqi main defensive zone around Karbala.

These were the battles the U.S. forces had practiced again and again in computer-assisted war-gaming at the U.S. Army's National Training Center in the Mojave Desert, and in the prewar battle planning at unit level. The theory was simple: Detect the enemy early; attack from a distance using air-delivered fire and artillery to gain maximum advantage; close with the enemy only after he's been thoroughly pummeled. But in practice the operation is always harder—the terrain alarmingly unfamiliar, the dust, the noise, the sudden shock of contact. Even advanced technology can't remove all the effects of the terrain, where unanticipated folds in the ground can conceal enemy forces, or minefields, or a ditch that can't be crossed.

But in this case the theory worked. It was about patience, surprisingly. Approaching U.S. elements spotted the force and used artillery and A–10 close-support aircraft to engage and destroy it, striking again and again over a few hours until there was nothing left of the Iraqis. It was the kind of fight that would have made the observer-controllers at the National Training Center proud. Meanwhile, the division's other elements, most on the move and running hard to keep up, continued to close toward the front.

Having cleared out the enemy's security zone, the lead elements of the 3rd Infantry Division rolled forward onto the escarpment and then farther north toward the so-called Red Zone—the enemy's main defensive positions in the large arc around Baghdad (see map). And behind them were elements of the second U.S. Army division, the 101st Airborne, truck-mounted, moving to set up staging areas for their helicopters so they, too, could join the battle. Meanwhile, special forces reconnaissance teams, airborne sensors, and UAVs were used to target the Iraqi ground forces.

If the Iraqis had learned from their Gulf War experience and from the Serbs, they would carefully conceal their forces, disperse, and blend into the built-up areas where they were less detectable and more difficult to strike. If they were disciplined, they would fight in small units, netted together by wire communications and overlapping fields of fire. And most of all, they would appreciate that their mission in the face of U.S. airpower

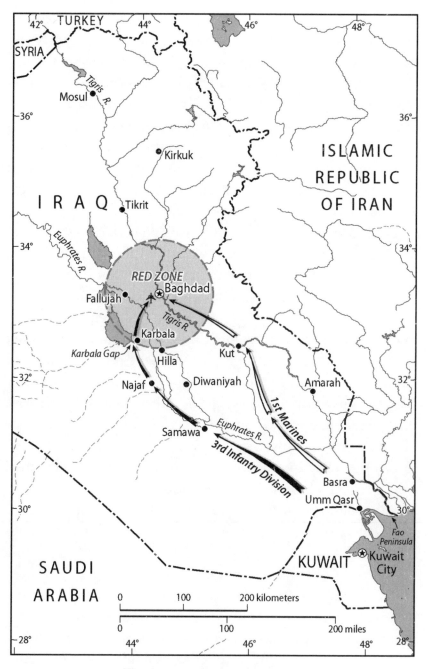

The Approaches to Baghdad

was simply to survive. In this way, there would still remain the possibility of a tough fight at close range against U.S. forces on the ground, either on the approaches or within Baghdad itself.

The question was, "What had the Iraqis learned over the preceding decade?" In the Red Zone four Iraqi Republican Guards divisions were occupying a semicircular defensive zone some fifty miles around Baghdad. In the southwest was the Medina Armored Division, in the center the Hammurabi Mechanized Division, and on the east the Baghdad Infantry Division and the Al Nida Division.

Each of these divisions should have numbered around 10,000 troops. The armored division, Medina, had about 250 tanks, 250 wheeled or tracked armored fighting vehicles for infantry, and perhaps 60 tubes of artillery. But some of the equipment would have been inoperative, and officers and troops would have begun to feel off-balance, then demoralized. So the combat wouldn't have been weapon against weapon—and the results couldn't be predicted that way. Rather the Iraqis were being set up: They were the opposing force, and if the Americans had their way, then just about every weapon in the U.S. arsenal was going to be brought to bear against these Iraqi forces before they could even place a U.S. vehicle in their sights. By that time much of the Iraqi weapons would be destroyed; their leaders dead, wounded, or in retreat; their hopes for reinforcement dashed; soldiers on the left and right fleeing or out of action. This was not going to be a "fair fight." And it would start with the U.S. pilots and UAVs hunting out Iraqi positions on the ground.

Some Iraqi forces were hidden under the palm trees and against buildings, or arrayed under camouflage netting, but other elements were exposed, out in the open. And there was a steady trickle of movement from the Iraqi forces—some loaded on military trucks, some scattered in convoys, some in commercial or civilian vehicles—as they tried to sustain, prepare, and reposition forces to meet the rapid U.S. onslaught from the southwest. Exposed positions and movements were detectable. They could be seen. And what could be seen could be hit—this was the reality of high-tech warfare.

Airpower didn't necessarily destroy entire units instantly—although it could if it caught Iraqis on the move or concentrated fire on a tight defensive position—but even dug in and dispersed forces, once detected, faced an inexorable end. Pass by pass, strike by strike, individual vehicles could be hit, positions destroyed, and units scattered and eventually eliminated. The planes could attack from such high altitudes, and with such accuracy, that individual units simply had no defense. The initiative lay with the U.S. pilots.

But the U.S. commanders also knew that a rapid ground advance on a narrow front, even if supported by airpower, is a classic prescription for trouble in warfare. In 1944, in the frantic effort to cross the Rhine, Allied armies attacked along a single highway over numerous rivers. Memorialized as *A Bridge Too Far* in book and film, this Allied effort was a bold risk. And it failed, with the loss of thousands of Allied airborne troops.

By Sunday night, in the race to Baghdad, the risks were apparent, for there was trouble in the bypassed areas and those reported to have been already secured. In the west, a team of U.S. Army support elements from the 507th Maintenance Company took a wrong turn, leaving the well-traveled Highway 1, and instead found themselves disoriented and headed into the town of Nasiriyah. This was an outfit of "wrench-turners"—armed soldiers in unarmed and unarmored vehicles like Humvees and trucks. It was a scene that repeated the experiences of a hundred peacetime exercises—small rear-echelon support units, straying off course, out of communication, blundering into the enemy. Yet it was a problem that was known but had never been fixed, because the Army was chronically short of the necessary communications, weapons, and training time.

As they backtracked to get away from Nasiriyah, they were met by a fusillade of small-arms and rocket-propelled grenade fire from irregular forces and two tanks. Some vehicles escaped, including the commander's Humvee. Most didn't, however, and a few hours later a number of the troops turned up on Iraqi TV, some wounded, some dead, several with gunshot wounds to the head. It was the biggest American reversal of the war.

And in the same area, on the other side of town, U.S. Marines suffered ten killed—mostly from so-called friendly fire from a U.S. A–10—with scores wounded from the daylong battle. Trying to follow along the right flank of the U.S. Army forces, the Marines' passage through Nasiriyah became a six-hour battle. When it was over the Marines reported destroying ten T–55 tanks, artillery, and antiaircraft guns. But U.S. forces had gained a new respect for the determination of some of the Iraqi irregular units. There was an intensity to the resistance against the overwhelming American capabilities that was simply unexpected.

Even in the south, Marine and British forces were still having to fight around Basra and Umm Qasr, days after it had been reported that Umm Qasr had fallen to the coalition attack. In fact, Iraqi irregulars were counterattacking near Umm Qasr. And it turned out that some members of the 51st Division, rather than surrendering, had fallen back into Basra, where a tank and artillery battle raged on the outskirts. As the chairman of the U.S. Joint Chiefs of Staff noted on television, "Clearly they are not a beaten force."[1]

According to U.S. Army doctrine, the operation in Iraq should be viewed as three distinct but interrelated "fights" at each command echelon: *deep*, *close*, and *rear*. And these three fights had to be worked simultaneously. Whether a captain leading a company of ground-pounders, or a three-star general commanding all ground forces in the battle, operations are always organized as deep, close, or rear. Only the scale and the means are different. For the company commander, the deep fight might mean calling in mortars or artillery in front of his position; the close fight might be maneuvering platoons around the enemy's flank; and the rear fight might be a supply sergeant returning fire against a sniper as he brings the supplies forward. At the corps level, deep fights employed air strikes and attack helicopters, supported by long-range rockets, and the close fight was won by maneuvering divisions. The corps's rear battle might also be fought by specially designated units.

This approach provided one way to think about the operation and freed the U.S. military from the old ideas of the "front line" and a "safe rear." With this thinking it had finally broken the chains of World War I–era thinking. The military was able to maneuver and take risks, to extend the fight into the enemy's rear, and to guard against shock if struck from behind.

In the larger picture the actions in Nasiriyah and Basra were rear fights. And unless the Iraqis could totally shut down the flow of U.S. supplies and force the diversion of the main U.S. effort, then they were of no more than tactical significance—the strategic key remained Baghdad and its Republican Guards. And the commanders at all levels were schooled to maintain that focus until absolutely forced by circumstances to deviate.

On Monday morning the United States pressed the deep fight against the Republican Guards, this time with the first-ever

Corps-level "deep attack." Long studied and practiced, deep attacks are designed to bring the awesome killing power of the Apache helicopter—each able to carry as many as sixteen Hellfire antitank missiles—to bear against enemy tanks, trucks, and artillery before those forces can impact the ground battle.

During the hours of darkness, some thirty-two Apache helicopters launched toward the Medina Division, positioned astride the approach to Baghdad. The Apaches were targeted on command posts, armor, and artillery.

But the Iraqis spotted the Apaches as they flew over populated areas, alerted the Fedayeen, and began to engage the aircraft with small arms and rocket-propelled grenades. The Apaches initially did not return fire against the populated areas from which the enemy fire was coming. Perhaps a dozen tanks, artillery, and command vehicles in the target area were struck by Apaches. But the choppers took heavy and sustained fire, one was forced down and its two pilots later captured, and almost all the aircraft were damaged by ground fire. It was a troublesome postscript to Sunday's challenges.

On Monday, March 24, the advance of the U.S. 3rd Infantry was slowed—its lead elements had penetrated the security zone of the Republican Guards main defense, and the decisive battle lay just ahead. It was time to solidify and expand the grip on the areas we had moved through and, before the advance to Baghdad, set the force: refuel, rearm, conduct final reconnaissance, tweak the battle plans, and position reserves to exploit success.

U.S. airpower was focused now on the Republican Guards, using B–52 strikes with conventional munitions ("dumb" bombs) where the enemy was massed or positioned in the open, and striking with precision weapons at individual fighting vehicles and positions where necessary. The technique was to designate "kill boxes," or areas on the ground over which U.S. aircraft would patrol and seek targets to strike. At this point, it appeared that most Iraqi forces were still dispersed and in hiding—due to some combination of surprise at the speed of the U.S. advance, fear of U.S. airpower, or delay in setting up defenses. As long as the Iraqis could maintain concealment, U.S. airpower would be relatively ineffective. For the United States, success was thus dependent on air-ground cooperation: The imminent approach of coalition ground forces would force the Iraqis to move to defensive positions; without the approaching ground forces, airpower alone would be only marginally effective.

As this decisive battle was taking shape, the struggle continued in the rear. In Nasiriyah itself, one regiment of Marines remained engaged with the hundreds of irregular fighters inside the city. Also in the south, Iraqi tanks pushed back into the Rumaila oil fields. And at the northern end of the Fao Peninsula a battalion of armor and mechanized infantry attacked British forces. More fighting occurred in Umm Qasr, where there was persistent sniping and resistance; minesweeping work in the channel there was also delaying the arrival of relief supplies.

Then the weather began to close in. With the onset of the forecasted sandstorm Monday night, winds accelerated to thirty to forty-five miles per hour, slowing movement, closing down long-range direct fires, grounding helicopter operations, and generally degrading all activities except for close-in fighting.

So ended the first phase of the war. It had been exhilarating initially—and largely successful. And by the morning of March 22, perhaps the best news was that, already, it was clear that much of the worst-case scenario wasn't going to happen. In the first place, U.S. troops wouldn't be hit by chemical weapons in the staging areas in Kuwait. Nor would Israel be struck by SCUDs launched from the airfields in western Iraq. Nor would the Rumaila oil fields be destroyed or cause a regional environmental catastrophe. But U.S. public opinion had begun to turn, as the difficulties, resistance, and unfortunate incidents began to be reported. The American public loved the troops and wanted an easy win—but when the going got tough, support began to weaken.

This was a tendency magnified by the broadcast media, which insisted on reporting an up-to-the-minute account, was prevented by security measures from reporting everything that was happening in the deep and close battles, and tended instead to focus public attention on the news that correspondents in the field could get. This included the attack on the officers, Iraqi missile strikes, a sympathetic personal view of the soldiers themselves, continued resistance in the cities along the Euphrates, and a discouraging report by a pilot after a battle. By its very nature, such reporting couldn't be "balanced"—but it was immediate and gripping. Not even the official headquarters spokesmen could really break out of the pattern, for they, too, were often protecting ongoing operations and other sensitive information. It fell to the analysts and commentators to try to put each event in context, and to shape the overall perspective of the campaign. And thus the media itself became a battleground in the strategic struggle for continued public support of the war. And in an odd way, this drew the Bush administration itself into a battle against many of the retired officers and experts who provided the running commentary.

In the midst of the storm on Monday night and Tuesday, March 25, the deep battle continued. Air strikes continued against Baghdad, including the intelligence complex and Iraqi Television. Aircraft and artillery continued to attack the Republican Guards in the Red Zone, too, even without good visibility.

And the sandstorm provided good cover for Iraqis in the continued rear fight, around the bypassed cities of Najaf and Samawah as well as in the south. Iraqi irregulars were continuing to work against the road movements necessary to sustain and advance the force, even in cities like Safwan, which was on the Kuwaiti border and supposedly liberated the first day of the war.

Meanwhile, the 1st Marine Division, delayed by a longer route and other tasks en route, continued to push northeastward toward the Baghdad Republican Guards Division positioned near Kut. This was tough ground over which to maneuver, crisscrossed with canals, groves of palm trees, and villages, far more complex than the Army's race across the open desert. And these Marines were operating with sizeable forces still committed to cleaning up and securing the situation in Nasiriyah.

By Tuesday, the degree of operational risk—the issue of whether the three-plus division-sized U.S. forces, supported by heavy airpower, would be adequate to smash the Republican Guards and seize Baghdad—was increasingly clear. And now the tone of the media changed, at least in the United States. Hopes for rapid victory faded, and criticism of the plans and adequacy of the force raged as commanders in the field admitted to having been surprised by the unexpected Iraqi tactics. Estimates of the numbers of irregular forces ran as high as 60,000. The early euphoria had given way to gloom over the U.S. battle deaths, the sandstorms, the probability that Saddam was still alive and in charge, and the repeated failures to secure Umm Qasr and begin the delivery of relief supplies. Still, U.S. public support hung solid.

Wednesday saw U.S. and British forces continue to struggle with the sandstorm, as they tried to keep their attention focused on setting the force for the fight against the Republican Guards while also dealing with the continuing problem of Basra. This was no "operational pause," however, for either side.

As lead elements of the U.S. 3rd Infantry Division continued preparations to move against the Medina Division, some elements of the Iraqi force apparently maneuvered and, using the sandstorm as cover, moved forward toward the U.S. division. In addition, elements of the Special Republican Guards also were on the move, taking up positions outside Baghdad and heading farther south to reinforce enemy resistance around Najaf.

The Iraqi maneuvers showed that, however accurate the air attacks on the Iraqi command centers, Iraq command and control had not broken down; clearly, orders were being issued and received. And given the difficulties that the 3rd infantry was facing along its supply line, and the substantial force it had diverted to fight in the bypassed cities along its route, the Iraqi move made tactical sense—but only if the Iraqi force could avoid U.S. airpower.

For the Americans the Iraqi maneuvers represented a golden opportunity to find and destroy the force from above 20,000 feet. U.S. commanders had been monitoring ground activity through the JSTARS systems, a large radar mounted on Boeing 727 jets that could "see" the ground more than 150 miles away and detect movement. With JSTARS cueing other systems, like UAVs overhead, reconnaissance satellites, or high-flying aircraft, Iraqi movements were almost certain to become fatal errors. U.S. and British planes were quickly diverted to target moving forces. A combination of precision strikes and strafing attacks by A–10s took a toll on the enemy force; much of one column of several hundred vehicles was reported destroyed.

Meanwhile, the 1st and 2nd Brigades, 3rd Infantry Division, remained engaged in heavy fighting around Najaf. This was part of the division's rear battle, but it raged for more than thirty-six hours, with U.S. forces using artillery and airpower as well as direct-fire weapons. At least 1,000 Iraqis were reported slain in the operation, with U.S. losses tallied at three armored vehicles and one tank crewman killed. And farther to the rear, along the division's supply line, there was also fighting near Samawah, southeast of Najaf.

In the east, another Iraqi force was also maneuvering south from Baghdad, attempting to reinforce elements opposing the advance of the Marines toward Kut. And like the other Iraqi columns, they were detected and engaged from the air. Meanwhile, the Marines had their hands full with their supply line, too. On Wednesday, another fight erupted near the bridges on the southern side of Nasiriyah. Fifteen Marine Humvees and trucks were destroyed in the fighting, with some 60 marines wounded. Each unit seemed to be fighting its own war as it passed through.

But as the sandstorm lifted late Wednesday, the long-awaited northern arm of the coalition force began to arrive. Parachuting in off C–17 transports, some 1,000 members of the 173rd Airborne Brigade reinforced an airfield secured by Kurds and U.S. special forces. The jump was a tactical choice—it was the fastest way to place 1,000 troops on the ground. Equipped with Humvees and trucks, armed with artillery and mortars, supplemented later by a few air-landed tanks and Bradley fighting vehicles, and able to draw on the full range of U.S. air support, the force was a welcome addition to coalition deployments and placed on the ground an additional weapon that could be used against the Iraqi forces north of Baghdad.

Still, this new force was in a difficult situation, and little was to be expected in the immediate future. It was confronting a force estimated to be as high as ten Iraqi divisions, including one Republican Guards division, as well as a terrorist threat from an Al Qaeda-affiliated group, Ansar Al Islam. This was another of the calculated risks: that the insertion of the force would energize the Kurds in the north and worry the Iraqis, and that the combination of U.S. airpower and smart tactics could prevent the Iraqis from attacking to destroy the small U.S. element.

By late Wednesday, as the storm was lifting, the heavy air strikes against Baghdad were ratcheted up. The largest bunker-buster bombs were used. A national communications network, including the main telephone exchanges and the information ministry, were hit. This marked an escalation, a determination to shut down Iraqi command and control, as well as an end to the dialogue with Iraqi commanders. If the information war had worked—and there were later indications that it had, at least in part—the price had been to let the Iraqis maintain some ability to control and maneuver their units. Now it was time to shut down Iraqi communications.

Simultaneously, air strikes against the deployed Republican Guards divisions were intensified. The Iraqis were moving forward to reinforce prepared positions and hiding positions, but they were moving nonetheless, and that made them vulnerable. As the skies cleared of dust, the laser-guided bombs and visual targeting of other weapons could again be used. At one point in the battle, more than 1,000 aircraft were moving through Iraqi, Saudi, and Kuwaiti airspace.[2]

For the highest-level U.S. commanders, the operation was coming together like a set-piece: The rapid advance of the American ground units was forcing the Iraqis to move. Iraqi movement then enabled U.S. airpower and long-range rocket fire to be more effective. And these strikes were going to enable the continuing advance of U.S. forces into Baghdad. Both the maneuver and the strikes were enabled by UAVs, other imagery, and electronic intelligence, as well as scouts and deep reconnaissance on the ground. It was the American's ability to synchronize firepower and maneuver that proved decisive.

Perhaps the nearest historical parallel had been the dominant U.S. airpower deployed over France in the days just before and after the Allies' Normandy invasion in World War II. During that historic invasion—D-Day, June 6, 1944—Allied tactical airpower ripped up communications, infrastructure, and units as German commanders attempted to respond. This had a devastating effect on the movement of German reinforcements into the battle area, and it gave the Allies time to set the beachhead and mass the forces necessary for the eventual breakout into the French countryside and beyond. The Germans fought back nevertheless, with antiaircraft fires taking their toll; German units moving at night and by indirect routes arrived into the battle area delayed but still battle-worthy. Almost sixty years later, the Iraqis outside Baghdad lacked the experience and discipline of the World War II German force. And faced with high-tech attacks, high-altitude precision strikes, both day and night, the Iraqi forces were going to have real difficulty in moving to engage the Americans.

The U.S. ground forces, meanwhile, continued to prepare for the assault on Baghdad. Commanders had known that the force would need time to recover from the dash into Iraq—sleep, checks of weapons, refueling and rearming, and "huddling" to prepare for the next steps in the operation were essential. But unanticipated was the intensity of the rear fight to keep U.S. supply lines open. The goal was to assemble five days of "consumables"—fuel, food, water, ammunition—before the assault began. Meanwhile, large elements of the 3rd Infantry Division remained deployed around Najaf, where they had cordoned off the city to prevent its reinforcement and were periodically engaged by Iraqi irregular forces. These included the Fedayeen and some Special Republican Guards troops—some of whom had slipped south under the air strikes and penetrated the cordon to reinforce the Iraqi effort originally in Najaf.

By Wednesday night it was becoming clear that the situation at Najaf would have to be resolved. It was distracting too much of the 3rd Infantry Division from its mission and threatening to become a grisly preview of what might unfold in Baghdad—urban warfare at its worst. Cordoning wasn't a solution.

As for the desperate Iraqis, their reckless tactics were no substitute for solid forces, effective command and control, and good leadership. The Iraqis couldn't actually stop the American advance, but they could make it more difficult and expensive. But for whatever reason they fought—whether fear of Saddam, fanaticism, or patriotism—they were causing delays and casualties.

This degree of resistance had not been anticipated, not here, en route to Baghdad. The Iraqi National Congress, the self-proclaimed government-in-exile, had promised that Shiites would welcome U.S. forces as liberators, some saying that the Americans would reach the outskirts of Baghdad without firing a shot. They were wrong. The American commanders had to adjust their plans: The response to the situation on the ground had to be thought through and the missions and timing adjusted accordingly.

The adjustments were the call of the ground commanders, Army Lieutenant General Dave McKiernan, commanding all land forces, the Marine commander, Lieutenant General James Conway, commanding the 1st Marine Expeditionary Force, and Lieutenant General William Scott Wallace, commander of V

Corps. There was no formula for this kind of decision—it was a matter of informed professional judgment. And the results would show in the success of the force and the losses it sustained. Such professional judgment was the payoff for these commanders' experiences (thirty years plus) in the U.S. armed forces. They had studied the weapons, the tactics, the men and women they led, the enemy; they were learned in military history; they all held advanced degrees; they would have risen to the top in government or business had they not chosen to wear the uniform. And they were "uptaking" vast amounts of information—simultaneous radio communications, spot reports, images on a dozen video monitors. They could visualize how the battle ahead might shape up. And they would weigh the alternatives to make the right call. Even more than the technology, it was these experienced, capable leaders, and the thousands of leaders who backed them up at every level, that gave the U.S. military its extraordinary capabilities. It was their dedication, their skills, and their judgment that would ultimately make the difference in battle.

In one of many efforts to maintain the focus and coordination of the force, Lieutenant General Wallace explained to his commanders and staff that "the enemy we're fighting is different from the one we'd war-gamed against." He was overheard, his comment picked up by the press and publicized. Thanks to the embedded media, this sparked a small crisis.

Wallace's comment underscored a rising tide of concern and criticism of the forces deployed, as well as the timetable for the operation that had been emerging from the press and commentators. The publicity hurled Wallace square against senior military and defense officials in Washington, who had been assuring all that everything was moving according to plan and right on schedule. This was "friendly fire," fratricide on the strategic level, as senior leaders were fighting to present the inevitability of Iraq's defeat and to maintain the pressure against Iraq in the information war. Their reaction was strong and immediate.

The Bush administration insisted that everything was fine. General Richard Myers, chairman of the Joint Chiefs of Staff, said, "No plan, no matter how perfect, survives first contact with the enemy ... but the plan is sound, it's being executed, and it's on track." But the administration did acknowledge that it was moving additional forces to the theater—always part of the plan—totaling perhaps an additional 100,000 troops.

Secretary of Defense Donald Rumsfeld not only defended the conduct of the war but also followed up with another message: warning Syria and Iran that providing military supplies to Iraq or otherwise interfering with coalition operations would be viewed as "hostile acts."

Syrian and Iranian intervention would be a problem for the coalition, one that should have merited concern throughout the planning process—and it would be a good idea to warn the Syrians and Iranians to stay out of the conflict. The strong comments made headlines, diverting some press attention from criticism of the war. If Secretary Rumsfeld's comments were timed to reinforce to the public the grave risks we faced, as well as to warn away potential adversaries, they certainly succeeded.

But it was a reminder of the delicate balance that democracies must walk during wartime, and the special responsibilities that political leaders must bear not to abuse their trust, by using the need to protect classified information or conduct diplomacy, to manipulate opinion at home. For in such circumstances, the normal give-and-take, the checks and balances of peacetime, can break down—and the extraordinary reliance of a people on its government must be matched by equally extraordinary care in retaining the opportunities for information, debate, and even the criticism that come with democracy. Unlike the ancient Romans, we Americans have no system to end democracy in wartime. Thankfully, we never have and never will see the need to do so and elect a temporary dictator during war, and thus far we have seen no reason to do so.

The incident raised internal Army problems as well, for it might have appeared to the Pentagon that Wallace had lost confidence. Here was where the Army leadership proved its mettle, privately defending Wallace's comments and leadership—and the crisis soon blew over. But when Secretary Rumsfeld pointedly emphasized in briefings that "the war plan is Tom Franks' war plan," it was a stark reminder that in military operations, no matter the right and authority of the civilian political masters to shape and develop the plan, it's the military that will ultimately be held accountable. That it is why the senior military commanders must be strong enough and clear-thinking enough to insist on the military essentials in any operation.

Wallace was calling it straight in a private dialogue with his commanders—the resistance in the southern cities had not been expected. Adjustments were required to deal with it, and the fact that the adjustments were being made was less a credit to the plan than to the high-quality leadership and robust communications that the American forces enjoyed. But neither was it a criticism of the plan, for such adjustments have to be expected in any operation.

The commanders determined that the 3rd Infantry Division should pass off the problem to another unit. The 1st Brigade, 101st Airborne, was diverted to the area, with the aim of eventually enabling 3rd Infantry elements to slip north and focus on the coming fight around Baghdad. Enemy resistance in Samawah had also been turned over to the 101st to deal with. This was a textbook assignment for a "follow and support" division, but no Army staff officer would have picked the 101st—a force organized and equipped for long-range, high-mobility operations—if there had been any other choice. Moreover, it diverted the 101st from participating in the assault on Baghdad. The last of the reserve elements—2nd Brigade, 82nd Airborne, previously held for an airborne assault against Saddam Hussein airport in Baghdad—was also committed to securing the supply routes.

So the risks were raised again: There would be only two American divisions available to attack the Republican Guards and seize Baghdad: the Army's 3rd Infantry Division and the 1st Marine Division. From the strategic level, General Myers and Secretary Rumsfeld's contention that the plan was on track was substantially correct—the ultimate focus remained on Baghdad as the enemy's center of gravity. The force had in fact moved well, averted the earlier disaster-type scenarios, and was on track to accomplish its objectives, albeit a little behind the best-case estimates and with greater risk.

Wallace remained in command and the battle moved forward, but the incident was a burr for an administration that worked hard to produce a winning image—not only for its politics at home but for the overall success of the campaign. It was a powerful reminder of the sensitivity of public opinion and the complications of what the Pentagon called "information war." Maintaining public support seemed to require projecting a winning image—and so anything that detracted from that could be viewed as harmful. Some within the armed forces were enamored with what they saw as a new concept, when in reality it was no more than a new label obscuring old questions: Does truth or propaganda best serve the overall public interest during war? In our democracy, we believed we had already resolved that issue during World War II, Korea, and Vietnam—that honesty is the best policy, even in wartime. After all, that was one of the great benefits of embedded media.

The military plan continued to progress on Friday and into Saturday. Air strikes hammered the Iraqi communications networks, as well as sites near the information and planning ministries. As the Iraqi air defense system crumbled, for the first time U.S. commanders were able to employ a combination of B–1, B–2, and B–52 bombers against targets in and around Baghdad. With four telephone company exchanges hit, telephone service was at last disrupted in the city and among Iraqi military commanders.

An unexplained explosion also struck a marketplace in Baghdad, marking the first significant numbers of Iraqi civilians killed or injured in a single strike. The Iraqis charged it was an American bomb; the Americans countered that it was probably an errant Iraqi missile. Regardless, the airwaves overseas began to be dominated by pictures of dead and wounded Iraqi civilians. It was the kind of incident that can alter policy and interfere with missions. It fed the rising tide of anti-American opinion within Europe and the Arab world. Coupled with the setbacks of the sandstorm, fighting along the supply line, and discouraging reports in the press, this event by itself presented an additional threat to the overall U.S. effort.

And the differences between the messages carried by international media and the U.S. domestic media was already a problem for the information war. The presence of embedded journalists, coupled with the release of only minimal details on the air campaign, kept the U.S. media focused on the ground campaign. But

the foreign media, especially the Arab media, were less interested
in the American forces than in the people of Iraq. Outside the
United States, scenes of the marketplace casualties sparked
intense concern, while at home the polls still showed very solid
support for the war, even if it were to require many months and
entail continuing losses.

Meanwhile, more than 700 sorties of fighter jets, bombers,
and attack helicopters flew against Iraqi ground forces, about 80
percent aimed at the Medina, Hammurabi, and Baghdad Divisions defending Baghdad. For the first time, the attack helicopters of the 101st joined in the fight, conducting a superbly
organized deep attack mission against elements of the Medina
Division near Karbala. And in this mission the appropriate lessons were taken from the first of the Apache deep strikes. The
helicopters went in as part of an integrated Army and Air Force
effort, they avoided overflights of populated areas, and their
rules of engagement permitted them to defend themselves by
returning enemy fire, even if it came from populated areas.
Simultaneously, ground elements of the 101st were still in the
process of taking the handover from the 3rd Infantry Division of
the fighting around Najaf and preparing to extend to Karbala, as
the latter focused on preparing to attack into the Red Zone.

Farther south and east the Marines continued their move forward, still engaged in a running fight in and around Nasiriyah.
In the far north, U.S. special forces teamed up with Kurds and
U.S. airpower to attack and destroy the Ansar Al Islam base,
killing several dozen radical fighters and running many more
back over the border into Iran. The results were a welcome surprise, as the Islamic fighters' resistance quickly folded under the
pressure of the air strikes.

On Saturday, March 29, the Iraqis added suicide bombing to

their means of resistance. The 3rd Infantry Division was still attempting to disengage from Najaf when an Iraqi taxi driver summoned over four soldiers for assistance—and then exploded himself, killing four Americans. For the Iraqis, this was a strategic move, further changing the relationship between American forces and Iraqi civilians. Already wary of civilians because of the organized resistance of the Fedayeen and Iraqi soldiers who had shed their uniforms, now Americans were going to have to treat every encounter as a potential suicide bombing. At a minimum, there would be a need for standoff, but more fundamentally the suicide attack undercut the U.S. aim of trying to build rapport with the local populace. It was one more setback.

In the United States, over the weekend, the Bush administration continued to defend its planning for the war. Spokesmen denied that any changes were being made to the plan—a statement belied as deployment of the 2nd Armored Cavalry Regiment, a 2,000-man wheeled reconnaissance and security force ideal for supply route security missions, was accelerated and its equipment readied for air transportation to the theater, rather than the seaborne deployment prescribed in the plan.

The weekend saw full-court information warfare, with stories reporting that all the commanders had agreed with the plan before the start of the campaign, denials by the secretary of defense that it was his plan, appeals for patience, plus many explanations as to why additional forces would have impeded diplomacy or raised the risk. The commander was enlisted in the defense: "I did not request additional troops before the beginning," General Franks said.

The simple truth was that all along the plan had compromised between commanders on the ground—seeking more forces to reduce military risks—and leaders in Washington—

who saw the diplomatic, financial, and political risks that an early and heavy buildup could entail. There was nothing wrong in principle with the process, but ultimately the military plan would have to work, and this would depend in part on the enemy. After ten days of war, it was increasingly clear that some assumptions about the Iraqis were wrong in the plan. Some were fighting, not surrendering, and Shiites in the south were passive, not actively joining the fight against Saddam's forces. For the commanders in theater, winning required adapting to a new situation; for the leaders in Washington and London, winning was a matter of hanging tough.

The charges and countercharges about the plan continued in the print and broadcast media throughout the weekend. But the real answer would be found on the ground and in the skies over Iraq, where the next phase of the operation began to unfold.

CHAPTER 3

DECISIVE OPERATIONS

WITH THEIR FORCES arrayed initially with three divisions north of Baghdad and four south, Saddam Hussein and his generals played into American hands. Rather than drawing back into Baghdad and waiting for the Americans, they opted for a forward defense in the southern cities. And when it began to show the first signs of success, they made the mistake of reinforcing, stripping Baghdad of the commands and forces essential to mount a real urban defense there. First elements of the Special Republican Guards were deployed forward to reinforce the Fedayeen. Then the Republican Guards divisions positioned north of the capital began to move south—ignoring whatever threat the small U.S. airborne forces inserted near Kirkuk might provide—and into the teeth of U.S. airpower, trying to reinforce a forward defense fifty miles outside Baghdad that was under sustained attack from coalition airpower.

The Iraqis placed their precious ground forces squarely in harm's way. It was only a matter of how long it would take—a day, a few days, a couple of weeks—before the ground forces hunkering down to escape the airpower were largely destroyed. If they remained in defensive areas, they would eventually be detected, either by manned aircraft circling overhead and staring downward into assigned "kill boxes," or by UAVs like Global Hawk, which could loiter overhead for more than twelve hours, passing back real-time television and targeting information that could be used to vector in the strike aircraft. Even routine logistics movements, as well as reinforcements by civilian vehicles, were being detected.

The airpower theorists, men like retired Air Force colonel John Warden and his advocates, were being proved right, but in ways they had not predicted. They had believed that airpower could win at the operational level of war by rapid knockout blows against the enemy's command and control systems. Airpower was decisive in a direct attack against the enemy's center of gravity, they would explain, whereas the army was fighting "at the tactical level," pecking away at the outer edges to try to reach the enemy's center of gravity. The reality was almost the opposite—but equally dazzling. Airpower, as part of a balanced air-ground team enabled by superb intelligence, was winning against the enemy's ground forces, which could not deploy to defend without being attacked and destroyed from the air. The key was to get hold of the enemy's main forces with airpower and pound them. Then it would be the combined punch of the air and the moving, hard-striking forces on the ground that would overwhelm the defense and move quickly to seize the center of gravity.

Thus the synchronization of high-tech airpower with agile ground maneuvers was helping to revise the old soldiers' rules about the need for 3:1 superiority in ground forces for an attack. And airpower was to provide the cushion against the risks of unanticipated contingencies on the battlefield. And though the soldiers were right when they said that airpower couldn't "hold ground," it could in fact make it very difficult for the enemy to do so. Airpower had enabled relatively small and compact U.S. ground forces in Iraq to achieve extraordinary gains in ground combat.

But the land-force planners also had it right when they emphasized the need for high-quality, lethal, and protected maneuver forces. It was their ability to advance under fire without loss that enabled the advance. A few shots, from machine guns and rocket-propelled grenades, scattered resistance, including the occasional armored vehicle: The forces blew right through them. No previous U.S. force would have been so capable. Indeed, on the ground, though this had become an attack of two U.S. divisions—one Army and one Marine—against six to ten Iraqi divisions, each U.S. division was probably equivalent to three to four Iraqi divisions, in view of its superior equipment, training, logistics, and communications—even discounting the enormous effects of airpower. The troops were about to rewrite the tactical rulebook in their next advance. In short, this operation was growing in competence as the services learned how to integrate their capabilities more effectively.

Meanwhile, each passing day saw a deeper bite taken out of Iraq's communications and air defenses, as more and more telephone exchanges and command centers in Baghdad were struck. So Iraqi forces, once committed to the front line, were increasingly irretrievable.

On Monday, March 31, heavy air strikes again hit the capital region, returning to telephone exchanges and bunker systems previously targeted. And on the ground, both Army and Marine forces continued to advance, the Army to the west of the Euphrates, the Marines to the east. The only way to assess the results of the air efforts was to probe and push. The inability to assess results from the air, then retarget and restrike, was one piece of the airpower puzzle not yet fully resolved. Instead, U.S. forces would push toward Baghdad until they met resistance, at which time they would mass fires from aircraft, helicopters, and artillery, destroy any resistance, and keep moving.

By Monday, the Medina Republican Guards Brigade west of the Euphrates near Karbala had been struck so hard by airpower and attack helicopters that it was combat-ineffective—literally unable to present an organized defense. Some reinforcements from the Iraqi Nebuchadnezzar Division had moved south into the zone of the U.S. advance, but they too had suffered heavy losses from U.S. airpower in the process.

In this way the U.S. ground forces continued to advance. The lead elements of the 3rd Infantry Division had reached Hindayah, and the Marines, who had begun pushing north overnight, were roughly parallel a dozen or so miles to the east. Both outfits were chewing up the opposition. Supplies were getting through, albeit slowly, and the forward units already had much of the logistical support they required.

Although the Iraqi Fedayeen and irregular forces continued to offer resistance along the U.S. supply lines, the adjustments made by the Americans would handle the problem. The U.S. 101st Airborne Division, reinforced by armor and mechanized infantry from the 3rd Infantry Division, were engaged in three simultaneous operations to prevent further disruption to the supply lines: west, north, and southeast of Najaf. These were full-scale battles involving artillery, air support, and direct fire against dug-in prepared Iraqi defensive positions. Working their way into the outskirts of Najaf, the 101st advanced street by street, house by house, flushing Iraqi fighters and destroying enemy weapons. Farther south, the brigade of the 82nd Airborne Division and Marines were still engaged in similar activities along the corps supply route and in Nasiriyah. The U.S. forces were good with their weapons, often first to fire, but usually restrained.

Still, the impact of the taxi driver's suicide bombing in Najaf, on top of repeated engagements with men in civilian clothing, was by now felt throughout the force. Fingers were on triggers, not on trigger guards, and some officers were saying that civilians should be assumed to be combatants until proven otherwise. In both the Army and Marine areas, there were a few gruesome incidents in which civilians were killed, sometimes before they could have even known they were in danger. It was regrettable but perhaps unavoidable. This was now the tragedy of "close combat," and the soldiers' first right, as always, was self-defense. After the suicide bombing, self-defense took on new meaning.

Back in Kuwait, the first ships from the U.S. 4th Infantry Division finally arrived at the port to begin offloading. Held off the coast of Turkey since mid-February, these ships were met by the division's soldiers flown in from Fort Hood, Texas. Early estimates were that the first elements would not be ready to move into Iraq until around April 10. Were the resistance to prove tough, these reinforcements would be most welcome.

About 150–200 attack aircraft were continuously airborne over Iraq, striking Republican Guards units. Much of this was so-called tank-plinking—going after individual items of equipment, rather than massed formations—but the days of repeated strikes were taking their toll against an ineffective Iraqi defense. The key Republican Guards divisions guarding Baghdad were estimated to be below 50 percent effectiveness.

Still there were indications of an intact Iraqi command and control system. Iraqi forces were continuing to move and maneuver on the battlefields, despite their vulnerability to destruction by U.S. airpower. Postwar Iraqi accounts seemed to confirm that Saddam and his sons, Uday and Qusay, were still effectively in command and ordering Republican Guards forces forward into the teeth of U.S. ground and air forces. In seeing the advance of the American forces toward Baghdad, the Iraqis were "reading the battle" correctly, but they were slow to react. Moreover, in organizing a forward defense, outside the urban parts of Baghdad itself, they failed to capitalize on the inherent advantages every urban defender enjoys when facing a superior force—greater knowledge of the complex urban terrain, prepared obstacles to constrict movement and restrict fields of fire, concealed avenues for resupply, covered and concealed fighting positions, and clever ambush sites.

By Wednesday morning the U.S. thrust into Baghdad had begun. In the north, the reconnaissance in force had turned into a real battle, as lead forces of the U.S. 3rd Infantry Division used the covers of darkness and heavy air and artillery to push through scattered Iraqi defenses north and west of Karbala. Attack helicopters hovered over Razzazah Lake, northwest of Karbala, to deliver fire against Iraqi positions. This was the so-called Karbala Gap, where U.S. forces had anticipated the Iraqi Medina Division's main defensive positions. The gap was a narrow strip of land between a lake and the city, which would force the attackers to concentrate their forces and become more vulnerable to Iraqi artillery and possible chemical attacks. But the U.S. training, rehearsal, air preparation, and buildup of the forces worked: By dawn on April 2, the 3rd Infantry Division was through, without significant losses.

To the east, the Marines' main effort had moved north and then east, up Highway 7, attacking the Baghdad Division under cover of heavy air strikes and artillery that took out Iraqi tanks, personnel carriers, long-range artillery, multiple rocket launchers, fuel trucks, and radar systems. And with a stiff direct-fire battle, they crossed the Tigris in the vicinity of Kut, some 100 miles southeast of Baghdad. The intent was to penetrate the Iraqi defenses, destroying as much of the Baghdad Division as necessary, and rolling over it toward Baghdad, all the while using air- and artillery-delivered fires to pin down and bypass the Iraqi 10th Armored Division around Amarah.

British forces had also escalated the fight around Basra, gaining control of Zubayr, the largest town on the western approach, seizing additional territory north and south and fighting their way into the western suburbs of Basra itself. Iraqi forces continued to fight back, however, even launching short-range missiles at British forces. The Brits had fought a cagey fight around Basra thus far, picking and whittling away at the enemy's resistance, without actually conducting a main assault on the city. The idea was to take an indirect approach, undercut the regime and supporters, humiliate them, defeat them piece by piece, and then gain the support and confidence of the local populace. This would not only spare the civilians and the infrastructure from the ravages of war but also make the postconflict recovery much easier.

U.S. and British leaders remained concerned about the Iraqi chemical threat. But despite the warnings and alarms throughout the coalition command, no Iraqi chemical weapons had been used. In many locations chemical protective gear had been found, much of it in good condition, as though staged and ready for issue. But the weapons themselves were not to be found. None were delivered against Kuwait or the troops staged to enter the Red Zone, none found in the wreckage of the artillery and missile units taken out by U.S. firepower, or in the fortifications or ammunition bunkers waiting to be issued. Even as U.S. forces rolled north, no chemical weapons of any type were found in the suspected ammunition storage depots.

By late Wednesday, April 2, and into the early morning of Thursday the momentum was clearly back with the coalition.

Approaching Baghdad from the southwest, the 3rd Infantry Division was continuing its attack, fighting scattered engagements and moving through Iraqi artillery fire. Airpower, helicopters, and artillery had done their work here; the Iraqi defense had broken down, with units increasingly scattered and disorganized, reinforcing elements from the north and east were rendered ineffective, and Iraqi battlefield command and control was faltering. Keep in mind that this was the vaunted Republican Guards, the Medina Division, plus reinforcements from other forces, the Hammurabi and the Nebuchadnezzar Divisions.

For the United States, this was a "penetration" attack intended to get through and around the enemy's defenses. We had worked out such a maneuver for years in training centers and map maneuvers. Pick a spot and blow a hole in the defensive lines; get inside the enemy's main defense and then widen the gap; fight against his flanks and rear—no frontal assaults; overrun his artillery and command centers; keep him off-balance and stay inside his "decision cycle"; move and strike faster than he could react.

It wasn't as though these tactics were startling or new in principle. In World War I the Germans had begun to use what they called "Hutier tactics" to break open trench warfare (reconnaissance and infiltration using small-group tactics). German as well as Soviet forces had employed the penetration attack as a standard maneuver during World War II with great effectiveness. In fact, the U.S. Army fell victim to such German tactics at the infamous Battle of the Bulge.

But in 2003 in Iraq the tactics and the means belonged to us. Once U.S. ground forces could fix the positions of the Iraqi troop battalions, artillery, and headquarters, U.S. airpower and artillery strikes would blow apart any defenses. Then, the Americans would simply outfight the Iraqis on the ground, taking advantage of their better fighting skills and superior equipment, to make the penetration. Once through, U.S. Army and Marine forces had the command and control, the mobility, and the staying power to "exploit"—to push on through and go after the softer targets in the rear. Tempo was important: In theory a U.S. breakthrough could possibly find itself sealed off, and Iraqi defenses reformed, if the initial penetration wasn't followed quickly by aggressive exploitation. Commanders were taught to push forward as far and as fast as their logistics would permit.

The U.S. 3rd Infantry Division made its first penetration around Karbala, sweeping through the remnants of the force there. Of course, the battlefield hadn't been "cleared" of the enemy, and the area was still dangerous. A U.S. UH–60 Black Hawk helicopter was shot down near Karbala Wednesday night. But the advance of the U.S. forces was assured—the only issues were how soon and how far. A fierce fight with a dug-in Iraqi force around the six-lane highway bridge over the Euphrates some 20 miles from Baghdad lasted about three hours on Wednesday afternoon. Then, the U.S. forces went through. And rather than turning south, to take the Medina Division positions east of the river from the flank, the 3rd Infantry Division was able to turn north. The division worked throughout the daylight hours on Wednesday to push its forces forward across the captured bridge over the Euphrates and prepare to face the remnants of the Medina Division, the Hammurabi Division, or whatever else might lie ahead on the road to Baghdad.

By Thursday morning, the 3rd Infantry Division was within twenty miles of Baghdad. The 2nd Brigade advanced from its bridgehead over the Euphrates northeast to seize the intersection of Highways 1 and 8. And the 1st Brigade "exploited" north, overrunning scattered Iraqi defenders and seizing the Baghdad airport in the early evening hours of April 3. The division was engaged in a series of running skirmishes, striking at Iraqi forces who resisted its advance, then blowing past, leaving the Iraqis to be attacked by air and artillery, or to straggle over and surrender. It was classic exploitation against an enemy force defeated but attempting to retain the field of battle. By late evening the door to Baghdad was almost open, the only anticipated resistance being remnant Republican Guards from divisions that had fallen back, as well as some Special Republican Guards forces that were defending in the vicinity of the airport.

The other "prong" of the offensive—the 1st Marine Division—had also surged forward, crossing the Tigris at Numaniyah, in the vicinity of Kut, encircling the Baghdad Division and calling on its remaining soldiers to surrender. The Marines had no intention of entering Kut to dig out any soldiers who had melted away into the population. Instead the idea was to contain them and focus on getting to Baghdad. In any case, it seemed that much of this Baghdad Republican Guards Division, deployed in and around Kut, had been destroyed by air strikes and artillery—its soldiers missing from the battlefield.

The Al Nida Division lay a few miles ahead, on the route to Baghdad. But its forces were already under attack from Air force and Marine airpower, with B–52s as well as strike aircraft targeting them around the clock.

The bulk of the Marines moved up Highway 6 toward Baghdad, leaving a small part of their force to probe and contain Kut and Numaniyah, where they had found scattered resistance. Oncoming traffic was heavy with busloads of Iraqi civilians, as well as deserters fleeing south in surrender. But the Marines kept the pressure on identified enemy forces, targeting units near the village of Furat and blasting through the remnants of a tank battalion. This advance brought them to within fifteen miles of Baghdad.

Also supporting the attack on Baghdad were the Special Operations Forces. Early in the war they had seized positions commanding the airfields in western Iraq to ensure that no Iraqi SCUDs would target Israel. Then, as some moved elsewhere to search and attack in western Iraq, others had moved into Baghdad, where for some days they had maintained small elements inside the city itself, searching for high-value targets and calling in air strikes. Now they were reinforcing, cutting off highways to the north, attacking Saddam's palace at Tharthar, and seeking to scout and attack any centers of resistance or command and control.

Meanwhile, the "rear battle" continued along the supply line. In Najaf, soldiers from the 101st Airborne used artillery, attack helicopters, precision bombing, and skillful maneuver to drive back Iraqi fighters through the streets. Some Iraqi fighters took refuge in the shrine of Ali, one of the holiest sites in all of Islam, and used its cover to fire against Americans. There were scattered pockets of resistance elsewhere, with Iraqi fighters in civilian clothes attempting to blend into the population. For the first time in Najaf, though, some Iraqi residents began to welcome the Americans, pointing out paramilitary locations and warning of minefields. A few miles south, elements of the 82nd Airborne were mopping up in Samawah.

North of Baghdad, Iraqi forces continued to withdraw,

pulling back several miles from positions around the city of Mosul, after five days of intense air attacks directed by U.S. special forces, just as they had previously withdrawn from the vicinity of Kirkuk. The maneuvers were defensive, to attempt to consolidate in positions less exposed to air strikes, but they did show that in the north, at least, some of the Iraqi units still had effective command and control. And, of course, there was not yet a significant U.S. ground force there able to exploit their weaknesses or the effects of the bombing.

On the home front, the information war entered a new phase, as the euphoria of the first day began to seep back into the American print and broadcast media. The momentum had so clearly shifted in our favor, our forces were advancing so well, and losses had been so light that the public gloom over the previous weekend suddenly lifted. War was mostly about human drama, it seemed, and these soldiers and Marines, along with their "embedded" correspondents, were catapulting forward into Baghdad with stunning success. It was a heady atmosphere of nascent triumphalism—our superior equipment, but above all our superior people, overcoming the challenge of suicide bombers, fanatic defenses, and the long-anticipated resistance of the Republican Guards. No matter how astonishing the airpower, it simply couldn't fire the imagination in the same way as the moving, maneuvering, and fighting ground troops.

The Bush administration gained a huge lift, at home and abroad, from the success of the troops. The debate over strategy and troop levels faded at home. In Germany the federal chancellor, Gerhard Schroeder, began to move toward a recognition of the American effort. And across much of the world, scenes of bombing victims were being replaced by the startling advances of the Americans. Iraqi Television, which had broadcast intermittently over the past week, showed a videotape of Saddam

Hussein that seemed to verify his survival after the first strikes on March 19. But there was no escaping the powerful images of U.S. forces at the airport outside Baghdad that flowed around the world and into Iraq on Friday.

On Thursday night and into Friday morning 1st Brigade, 3rd Infantry Division, continued to fight for control of the Baghdad airport. This had been their key objective when they entered Iraq two weeks earlier. Now, having grabbed a foothold at the airport, they had to expand their control and secure themselves against counterattacks. Into Friday evening the Iraqis probed and pushed, as the brigade's reinforcements poured into the area and expanded the perimeter, searching buildings, hangars, and underground tunnels and beating back counterattacks with artillery and airpower.

2nd Brigade, 3rd Infantry Division, was coming up from the south, methodically clearing isolated enemy forces from towns and villages along the way. By Saturday morning they had located and overrun what remained of Medina Division headquarters, by now no more than a cluster of burned-out vehicles and Iraqis in civilian clothes. There was sporadic enemy contact as 2nd Brigade moved north toward Baghdad, but it was clear that "deep battle" had done its job, with shattered equipment and demoralized soldiers spread across much of the area.

3rd Infantry Division reported killing some 2,000 Iraqi soldiers in the drive across the Euphrates and up to the outskirts of Baghdad. And if airpower and artillery had opened the way, the maneuver forces were now critical, for as they moved and fought they destroyed any hopes that the Iraqi forces might reconsolidate and resume any substantial resistance.

Farther east the U.S. Marines found the going tough at times, encountering fanatical resistance in one village from foreign volunteers, mostly Egyptian and Jordanian, who executed an effective ambush, knocked out a tank, and inflicted casualties. Elsewhere the Marines rolled forward, destroying most of two brigades of the Al Nida Division, capturing more than 2,500 prisoners, and, in an intense three-hour fight with tanks and helicopters in support, routing the last of the effective Al Nida units from a strategic crossroads southeast of Baghdad.

The Marines advanced with a fierce passion, fighting in regimental combat teams with their own assigned fire support. Theirs was the most difficult route: across the Euphrates Valley before bridging the Tigris, then advancing on Baghdad from the southeast with two divisions stacked in depth against them. It had been a struggle to keep up with the Army, but the Marines had done so. It was a surprise, then, when the commander of 1st Marines Regimental Combat Team Colonel Joe Dowdy was relieved of command during the last push toward Baghdad. It was said that he lacked aggressiveness when his forces had been ordered to move forward in a feint to draw Iraqi artillery fire. Such decisions, made under the trying circumstances of battle, can be explained by any number of factors. This was a proud Marine force engaged in a sustained land battle for which it was not fully equipped, struggling on a much more difficult route to keep up with the Army forces to its left in the attack on Baghdad. And in the midst of such frustrations, unique circumstances and the respective personalities play out in ways difficult to predict or control. Still, Colonel Dowdy was the only senior officer of any service known to have been relieved during the fighting—a remarkable testament to the overall effectiveness of the armed services' command selection, leader development, and training programs.

By Saturday morning, as Army special forces continued to work deep inside Baghdad, an Army column—Task Force 1–64 Armor, 2nd Brigade, 3rd Infantry Division—was ready to execute the first daytime raid into Baghdad itself, a twenty-five-mile mounted probe that circled from an attack position south of Baghdad in through the city itself and then fought its way out to the west to the airport. It was, in spirit, pure cavalry schmaltz, the kind of bold daylight ride that might have been executed by J.E.B. Stuart during the U.S. Civil War. But it had "bite." It brought speed, firepower, and shock from mounted forces into the heart of the Iraqi capital. There would be no denying the presence of Americans in Baghdad.

This raid was essentially the brainchild of one American, Colonel Dave Perkins, commander of 2nd Brigade. He called the division commander, Major General Buford Blount, and expressed concern that we might be settling into a siege mentality; he asked permission, instead, to conduct the raid. It was individual insight and initiative, the product of Perkins's twenty-plus years of experience, a well-structured Army system of leader development, and a commander who had confidence in his team and the courage to support them. When Major General Blount assented and got corps approval, the mission was on.

As a column of more than forty tanks and Bradley fighting vehicles roared north on Hilla Road into Baghdad, it caught the Iraqis virtually unawares. Off-guard and out of position, they responded hastily and piecemeal, firing back at the armor with small arms, machine guns, and rocket-propelled grenades. But the column returned fire and maneuvered fiercely against 2,000–3,000 Iraqi fighters, running over vehicles and firing heavy weapons at close range, smashing any hope of mounting a cohesive defense of the city. Making its way out to the airport on the expressway, the raid further disrupted any Iraqi ambition to counterattack 1st Brigade's positions there.

The intent was not to seize key points or hold the ground, but rather to penetrate, reconnoiter, and disrupt, trying to prevent any real urban battle if possible. All that was accomplished. The raid marked another upward ratchet in the continuing escalation of U.S. military dominance of the Iraqi forces. It also established the impression of U.S. military success—for this was the fundamental truth in information war: Actions and images are more powerful than words.

Over Baghdad, meanwhile, U.S. forces were taking advantage of weakened Iraqi air defenses to fly UAVs, the Hunter and Predator drones, to track enemy and friendly movements and provide pinpoint targets. Working together, and able to follow the action in real-time via TV cameras placed aboard the drones, U.S. forces could overcome one of the principal advantages of any urban defense: the isolation of various units and battlefields within a city. Now the United States could see it all—and react anywhere.

In the north, special forces with the Kurds had maintained steady pressure on the Iraqis, forcing them to fall back, calling in air strikes to inflict casualties, and dodging Iraqi return fires and counterattacks. But here the Americans with the Kurdish allies were the lighter, less capable force, and airpower alone kept them in the fight and kept them safe from real harm. Still, the Iraqis put up a tough fight, counterattacking and then falling back only under pressure.

Moving forward against Iraqi resistance, U.S. special forces and Kurds were calling for repeated air strikes. And here occurred the worst of the conflict's several fratricide incidents. As the Kurds were moving forward, two U.S. aircraft mistakenly struck the column, killing one American, at least seventeen Kurdish fighters and a BBC translator, wounding perhaps another forty-five.

Friendly fire has always been a hazard of war, and nothing

shatters morale and breaks momentum like being struck by one's own forces. During the 1991 Gulf War, there had been several incidents of friendly fire, leaving embittered, angry units and leaders when the errors were discovered. Consequently, extensive measures had been taken to reduce friendly-fire incidents during this campaign. With the Global Positioning System (GPS) being widely used, both air and ground elements knew their own locations better than ever before. Satellite-relayed communications provided the means for ground-based controllers to contact air headquarters; ground-air communications between controllers and aircraft was also used extensively. Aircraft and missile batteries were equipped with Identification Friend or Foe transponders, which replied with a coded signal to interrogation.

Already in the war, U.S. Patriot missile batteries had shot down a British plane, and perhaps an American plane as well. One U.S. aircraft had struck a British armored vehicle in the south. Two British tanks had engaged each other, destroying one and killing its crewmen. An American A–10 had probably killed nine U.S. Marines and wounded as many as thirty in a mistaken strike in Nasiriyah. These latest strikes had not only wounded the local Kurdish leader but also shattered the momentum of the Kurds' U.S.-assisted advance toward Mosul.

But the main effort was in Baghdad. On Sunday, U.S. forces tightened their cordon around the city, with 3rd Infantry forces moving northward and eastward, spreading out from the airfield to block major roads entering the city and to link up with the Marines as they moved forward also. Both forces encountered isolated resistance, including some incidents of stubborn Iraqi defense. The Marines were advancing under the cover of their own artillery and rocket fire, but for the first time they had to

cope with a successful Iraqi demolition of a bridge. It was a con-
fusing and cluttered battlefield environment, with abandoned
Iraqi equipment and fleeing forces, as well as thousands of Iraqi
civilians trying to escape the battle area. But by the end of the
day, the combination of Army, Marine, and special forces had
been able to block all the major avenues whereby Iraqi reinforcements might enter the city.

Iraq's information minister continued to claim that the U.S.
attack had been foiled, asserting that U.S. forces at the airport
were surrounded. And indeed, his public statements generally
mirrored the intercepted reports that U.S. intelligence teams had
monitored being sent to Saddam's son Qusay. One of the ironies
of this war was that the incorrect Iraqi reporting, apparently
deliberately falsified by Iraqi officials in order to avoid "shoot the
messenger" reprisals, may have done as much as U.S. counter-
command and control efforts to undercut the Iraqis. Despite the
lengthy U.S. effort to undercut the regime's information operations, take its broadcasts off the air, and eliminate Iraqi command
and control, the Iraqi government was still issuing false reports
and disputing the facts on the ground. It was one more illustra-
tion of the extraordinary difficulty of "counterregime" targeting
and attacks on strategic command and control.

On Monday morning, April 7, U.S. forces again rolled into
Baghdad. The Marines were forcing their way over the Diyala
River and moving toward the center of Baghdad from the east,
working their way against stubborn resistance. And from the
south most of the combat elements of 2nd Brigade, 3rd Infantry
Division, some seventy tanks and sixty other armored vehicles,
fought their way into and occupied the Republican Palace (Iraq's
official seat of government) and the residential Sijood Palace.
The advance was fiercely contested by infantry dug in at inter-

sections and maneuvering on foot from building to building, demonstrating at least local command and control. And underscoring the remaining fight, an Iraqi rocket strike hit and destroyed 2nd Brigade's tactical operations center. There was also tough fighting around the Rashid Hotel, the Ministry of Information building, and the parade ground.

Yet U.S. leaders knew that Iraqi resistance would collapse even sooner if Saddam Hussein could be taken out, and so the U.S. forces remained in hot pursuit.

Reportedly, Saddam was being followed by at least one CIA-recruited spy and a Delta Force commando. On Monday afternoon multiple sources reported that he had entered a restaurant in a Baghdad suburb.[1] A single B–1 bomber, already overhead, was given the target coordinates and struck with four 2,000-pound bombs, two of which were bunker-busters, within forty-five minutes. Again there was hope that Saddam and his sons had been hit. Also on Monday night, special forces raided another area of the information ministry, in one more attempt to destroy the center of Saddam's information operation.

But Tuesday morning saw Iraqis mounting a fierce series of counterattacks to recapture the presidential palace complex on the western bank of the Tigris River. Moving in about fifty trucks, buses, and armored fighting vehicles, the Iraqi forces were a mixture of Special Republican Guards, Fedayeen, and Baath Party loyalists. A visible threat as they moved toward the bridges, the Iraqi forces were first hit with air and artillery fires. Most made it across the bridges and closed with forces of 2nd Brigade, 3rd Infantry Division, which had been deployed to protect U.S. positions around the palace complex. There the Iraqis were simply overmatched by the tanks and Bradley fighting vehicles, which could hold their ground and deliver sustained and devastating fire. Many of the Iraqis scattered on foot and attempted to enter buildings on the western bank to use as sniper positions. But here they were simply picked off, location by location, by air, artillery, and mortar fires. There were also at least three attempted suicide bombings, with the explosive-laden cars being engaged and destroyed well beyond lethal range. By late afternoon, the counterattack on 2nd Brigade's position had been defeated. And for the first time, U.S. aircraft were operating at low altitudes over the capital city, delivering accurate strikes on buildings and armored vehicles; one U.S. aircraft was shot down by an Iraqi Roland missile.

Though the Iraqi information minister, Al Sahhaf, continued to deny it, this was indeed the end of the regime. Two additional brigades of 3rd Infantry Division were advancing into Baghdad, with 3rd Brigade circling around to enter from the north, and 1st Brigade moving eastward from its base at the airport. By nightfall, the western bank of the Tigris was largely in U.S. hands and silent. After Monday's strike at Saddam, many Iraqi ministers had not reported to their offices, and by the end of Tuesday many Iraqi government buildings were in U.S. hands. Finally, Iraqi Television went off the air permanently.

The Marines, meanwhile, continuing their attack across Diyala River, had fought several stiff engagements, seized the Rashid airbase in eastern Baghdad three miles from the Tigris, and were continuing to advance. By Wednesday, when the Marines pushed forward to the eastern bank of the Tigris and linked up with 3rd Infantry forces there, the battle for Baghdad had been decided. There was still scattered fighting, but the streets were empty, and the grip of the Fedayeen was broken.

To the south, 101st Airborne had completed its work in Hilla, finishing up its "rear battle" responsibilities, and farther south in Basra the British grip was secure.

To the north problems remained, including the Iraqi troops in Kirkuk, Mosul, and Tikrit, but theses forces were under attack from the air. And with the fall of Baghdad, centralized Iraqi command and control was certainly broken; the defeat of these Iraqi forces was merely a matter of time at this point.

The fall of Baghdad took only seven days, from the rush to seize the airport on Thursday night, through to the end of organized resistance on Wednesday. As urban battles go, this one was unusual. Instead of long, drawn-out infantry fights from cellar to cellar, the battle for Baghdad was punctuated by crisp armored maneuver and relatively long range small-arms, cannon, mortar, and artillery fire. Precision airpower was surprisingly useful. And what some might have expected to be a fight of several weeks was effectively finished in less than one. What happened?

In the first place, Iraqi forces seemed surprised that U.S. forces were so close, despite the U.S. penetration in the vicinity of Karbala and across the Euphrates two days earlier. U.S. actions consistently took Iraqi defenders by surprise and caught them off-guard. Second, western sections of Baghdad were wide open and accessible to heavy armored vehicles, depriving the Iraqis of any close-quarters advantage they may have found elsewhere and favoring the U.S. forces. So by this point clean organizational lines had probably broken down, and the Iraqis' ability to coordinate fire and maneuver was limited. Many Iraqis fought hard and selflessly, but their preparations were poor, with little in the way of barricades, antitank ditches, extensive minefields, ambush positions, sited and concealed heavy weapons, and the other techniques common to successful urban warfare. For their bravery, Iraqis paid with their lives. Counterattacks merely hastened the end. More fundamentally, the Iraqis lacked, or had lost, the ability to plan the fight and shape the battlefield, which is the essence of defensive battles, especially urban ones.

Against these Iraqi deficiencies we can identify overwhelming U.S. strengths. Air supremacy gave attacking U.S. forces access to real-time intelligence, including full-motion video, as to Iraqi movements. The destruction of Iraqi telephone exchanges no doubt forced the Iraqis into easily overheard radio communications. And the United States took advantage of its overwhelming superiority to seize the initiative and force the Iraqis to expose themselves to piecemeal destruction. Working in combination, U.S. tactics of armored movement proved decisive: penetrating the city's perimeters and forcing inferior Iraqi forces to come to them—the superior U.S. firepower on the ground; deploying M1A1 Abrams tanks and, for the Army, Bradley fighting vehicles with 25mm guns; undertaking precision strikes, which were available on call, promptly, from helicopter and Air Force elements orbiting overhead; and taking advantage of the remarkable agility and responsiveness of U.S. forces.

On Thursday, the Iraqi defense around Kirkuk gave way after a U.S. B–52 walked a string of bombs down an Iraqi position on a key ridgeline north of the city. Within hours, as Iraqi defenders fled, Kirkuk had been seized by Kurdish forces working with U.S. special forces. Kirkuk fell before U.S. 173rd Airborne Brigade, reinforced by tanks and armored fighting vehicles flown in from Germany, could launch its own attack.

On Friday, Iraqi forces quit Mosul. As in Kirkuk, the airpower, targeted by a few Americans on the ground, proved decisive. Just as in the fighting against the Taliban in Afghanistan in the autumn of 2001, U.S. special forces were able to maneuver local troops to exploit weakened and disorganized forces, but the primary weapon of war was special-forces directed airpower.

By Friday, an element of U.S. 1st Marine Division was moving north from Baghdad to overrun any Iraqi resistance at Tikrit,

Saddam's home area and the last holdout of Iraqi forces. And by Monday, April 14, the last resistance in Tikrit had been overcome. Meanwhile, 4th Infantry Division, now assembled from its journey from Texas, had begun moving north into Iraq. This marked the end of the large-scale conventional combat—twenty-seven days after the first U.S. forces crossed into Iraq from Kuwait.

At the end, many were calling Operation Iraqi Freedom a vindication of the war-fighting strategy as well as the Department of Defense's planned transformation of the U.S. armed forces. But the truth is more complicated.

Of course, the operation succeeded in destroying the Iraqi armed forces, seizing Baghdad, and ejecting the Hussein regime from power. But given the respective power of the U.S. and Iraqi militaries, the outcome was never in doubt. The plan provided the right basis for adapting to the exigencies of the operation. In fact, these adaptations—an earlier start, revised missions to handle Basra and the supply routes, changes of timing to cope with the sandstorm, the rush into Baghdad—and especially the continued focus on Baghdad and the Republican Guards arrayed around the city—were what enabled the basic plan to succeed so dramatically.

General Tommy Franks and his commanders adroitly used tempo to their advantage, pacing their advance on the ground to allow supplies to catch up and the rear battle efforts to grip the Iraqi forces, then accelerating the pace when it became clear that the United States had gotten inside of the Iraqis' decision cycle as U.S. forces crossed the Euphrates and Tigris Rivers and neared Baghdad.

But enough credit can't be given to the soldiers, Marines, sailors, and airmen themselves. Ultimately the operation succeeded because of the competence of the units—especially the men and women handling the weapons and equipment. In war, battles are ultimately decided at the bottom of the organizations—by the tank commander who acquires the target and lays the gun faster than his adversary, the fighter pilot who squints through the haze and picks up the camouflaged enemy positions on the ground, the truck driver who moves cargo over difficult terrain. Without a decisive edge in competence, the air forces could not have hit the Iraqi forces effectively on the ground, nor could the ground forces have advanced through the Republican Guards so quickly and with such light casualties. Higher commanders can lose a campaign, or they can set the conditions for success. General Franks and his subordinate commanders skillfully exploited the superior capabilities of U.S. forces. The capabilities and competence were largely there, quality that had been built into U.S. forces during the decades since the end of the Vietnam War. But the commanders' role was to shape it, tune it, and apply it to the situation at hand. This they did brilliantly. Still, the winning is done at the bottom, and that's where you find the heroes. And the commanders would be the first to say this.

Some further assessments must await a better understanding of the Iraqis' intentions, plans, and activities. For example, it would appear that Franks achieved strategic surprise as a result of U.S. deception, particularly in attacking before 4th Infantry Division was deployed and without any forces in northern Iraq. But Saddam's failure to more rapidly redeploy forces from north to south of Baghdad may have been due as much to his stubbornness or overconfidence. His failure to prepare the Baghdad defenses was likely the result of leadership incompetence, fear of admitting that forward defenses might fail, or the breakdown of Iraqi command and control under the weight of the U.S. assault, though no doubt he also failed to anticipate the timing of the U.S. attack.

Another major uncertainty is the impact of the psychological warfare campaigns. Measured by U.S. expectations, the campaign was less than fully successful: No large units surrendered. The effort to convince the Iraqi forces not to use chemical weapons was successful simply because they were never issued chemical weapons to employ during the campaign. And the discouragement that led so many Iraqi leaders and troops to simply melt away from their units before and during battle could be attributed, at least in part, to the fear of overwhelming U.S. military power as well as a lack of confidence in their own forces and commanders. Still, the e-mail messages, phone calls and voice-mails, leaflets, and visits reportedly had an impact, at least in setting the Iraqis' mind-sets for what could follow and in encouraging the disintegration of some units. The hard question is the cost of the psychological effort—in this case, it seems to have been the delay in destroying some Iraqi communications. But that was the proper tradeoff.

As for the larger information war, the military actions spoke louder than words in defending the plan and the effectiveness of the forces. Certainly American public opinion was solidly in support. In the Middle East, though, where we most needed to win hearts and minds, the information war failed to sway anti-American sentiment and, in fact, deepened ill feelings. Moreover, in the aftermath of the operations, the early failure to find any significant chemical or biological weapons threat undercut the hopes of establishing greater international legitimacy, though the discovery of the mass graves dating from the early 1990s and the establishment of an Iraqi Council somewhat offset the impression of American aggression and occupation.

Though the decisive phase of the operation was successful, there were also problems. First, the plan took what could be viewed as *unnecessary* risk because it skimped on the forces made available to the commanders. And while the level of forces proved adequate for defeating the Iraqi military, the whole idea in military operations is effectiveness, not efficiency. Military operations should not be run like businesses, which use predictable requirements and operating environments to minimize input costs. Combat, especially land combat, is one of the most unpredictable of human activities. It is inherently risky, with the risks usually resulting from factors that are improbable or cannot be foreseen. Therefore, sound logic dictates the need to minimize foreseeable risks before beginning any operations.

Additional forces were available—they were even on orders. Another combat division, an additional force for securing the supply lines, more trucks and supply units to provide the redundancy that the inherent inefficiency of military operations requires— each would have reduced risk. Some of the planners knew this; it was the issue at the heart of continuing tensions during the planning process. But they weren't deployed until it was too late.

By the time it became clear that Turkey wasn't going to permit the passage of U.S. troops, it was too late to position a fourth combat division in Kuwait. But at least 2nd Cavalry Regiment or additional military police units could have been airlifted in— instead of waiting until after the crisis along the supply lines five days into the war. It is difficult to believe that additional forces along the supply route would not have helped preclude the kind of mistake that cost the soldiers of 507th Maintenance Company their lives.

The plan's excessive risk became clear with the postcombat stage, and here the forces and capabilities were unequal to the task. It was the planners' job to have anticipated the various contingencies and make adequate provision for them, including the possibility of postwar Iraqi resistance to U.S. occupation. The "rolling start" philosophy, which seemed to emerge as much from continuing deployment problems as any strategic calculus, made this impossible. The result was a U.S. force at the operation's end that was incapable of providing security, stopping the looting and sabotage, or establishing a credible presence throughout the country—or even within Baghdad. The ensuing disorder vitiated some of the boost in U.S. credibility won on the battlefield, and it opened the door for deeper and more organized resistance during the following weeks.

On March 20, when combat began, the U.S. Marines had four regiments available. The U.S. Army had only seven combat brigades present in Kuwait—the three brigades each of 3rd Infantry Division and the 101st Airborne Division, and a brigade of the 82nd Airborne—and some of the 101st itself was not ready to go. By April 11, when Mosul and Tikrit fell, the number of Army brigades in Iraq had increased to nine, with the arrival of 2nd Cavalry Regiment and 173rd Airborne Brigade. On May 1 President Bush declared an end to substantial combat activities. By the end of May, the number in theater was up to seventeen Army brigades, with the arrival of 1st Armored Division, 4th Infantry Division, and 3rd Armored Cavalry Regiment, as well as a brigade from 1st Infantry Division. By then, the extended disorder left the ultimate success of the mission at increased risk, despite the extra forces that had belatedly arrived.

Some may contend that a "rolling start" is inevitable in a modern war—that building up a stronger force, or starting the buildup earlier, would have sabotaged attempts to find a diplomatic solution. But the administration's own announcements belie this concern. The deployments of forces were habitually announced long before the forces actually began to move, and their size was exaggerated, giving an impression of substantially greater numbers than would actually be engaged in fighting.

Others have suggested that the relatively small ground component was accidental, that Secretary of Defense Donald Rumsfeld's continued questions about the plan and deployments simply disrupted the process to such an extent that required forces weren't able to be delivered—and that eventually the commanders reconciled themselves to this, not wanting to face the secretary's wrath by raising objections. Still others have suggested that all of this was a result of Rumsfeld's insistence on holding down financial costs. That is, additional forces would be held back until they were clearly needed. And some have suggested that Rumsfeld was proving his point about the relative merits of special forces and airpower compared to the traditional army. As one officer remarked, "He just always wanted to go light on the Army ground forces—same as in Afghanistan." Perhaps all these factors contributed.

The second major criticism of the plan—a profound flaw—was in the endgame: It "short-changed" postwar planning.[2] Planning military operations in war must take into account planning for the aftermath. Army and joint theater planning always presents requirements in a kind of four-step minuet: deployment—buildup—decisive operations—postconflict operations. Destruction of enemy forces on the battlefield creates a necessary—but not sufficient—condition for victory. Victory means not the defeat of the opposing army but rather winning the follow-through operation to accomplish the aims and intent of the plan. In this case, the purposes, as enunciated by Secretary Rumsfeld, included ending the regime, driving out and disrupting terrorist networks, finding and eliminating the weapons of mass destruction, eliminating terrorist activities, and crafting conditions for Iraq's rapid transition to a representative government "that is not a threat to its neighbors." Achieving victory requires backward planning, beginning with a definition of postwar success and working backward to determine the nature of the operations required and the forces necessary.

And here the administration's focus and determination on winning the war in military terms seemed to undermine preparations for success after the country was occupied.

The administration explained the situation in postwar Iraq as a matter of assumptions that hadn't quite worked out, "that tended to underestimate the problem,"[3] that removing Saddam would remove the Baath threat, that large numbers of military and police would rally to the Americans, and that the bureaucrats would stay on the job.

In fact, the lack of preparations was partly a consequence of the decisionmaking and leadership within the Bush administration and partly the result of deeper forces and tendencies at work within the U.S. government and U.S. military. From the beginning, the "decisive operations" (how to defeat Iraqi forces) had taken priority over the postwar plan (how to achieve the real objectives in Iraq). Organizations like the Pentagon simply focused on their core expertise, the application of military power—rather than the broader requirements inherent in the situation. This was compounded by a continuing bureaucratic struggle between State and Defense, the first cautious and circumspect, the other determined to forge ahead seemingly regardless of the issues. This was a struggle that wasn't decided until January 2003 by the White House decision to give full postwar responsibilities to the Department of Defense.

Not that there was any real structure or organization to back up the military planning within the government itself. The U.S.

Agency for International Development (USAID), part of the Department of State, did contracts—it was no planning and execution organization itself. Any semblance of the structure that had pursued nation-building in Vietnam was long gone. The Army had established the Peacekeeping Institute at its War College at Carlisle Barracks, Pennsylvania, but the small group of dedicated instructors had been cut back repeatedly and was fighting a budgetary decision that would disestablish the effort. Congress had established the U.S. Institute for Peace in a burst of 1970s antiwar idealism, and it served as an important focus for discussion and scholarship—but there was no real analog to the Air Force's RAND, or the Navy's Center for Naval Analyses, or the Army's RAND Arroyo Center, each federally funded to think through the tough issues associated with the armed forces' missions. Nor was there a bureaucratic structure dedicated to investing billions every year to improve our capabilities in peace operations. And there were no analogs to the defense industries, with their armies of consultants and lobbyists to gain favorable appropriations.

Recognizing the problem, the Clinton administration had at least tried to create an interagency coordination mechanism that might bring together the full resources of the federal government in pursuit of a more sophisticated and comprehensive approach to dealing with post-conflict problems of the so-called failed states. Developed pragmatically from extensive preparations to provide an exit strategy for the 1994 U.S. military operation in Haiti, the process held each agency responsible for some portion of the nation assistance tasks and provided an interagency coordination process at the deputies level. It was essentially an expansion of the military staff planning and orders process to the full U.S. government, tasking departments to organize and accomplish certain tasks. The process became formalized as Presidential Decision Directive (PDD) 56, published in 1997. But even the process under PDD 56 was simply inadequate to the breadth and intensity of the challenges involved in dealing with the failed states problem.

As I went through the Pentagon to check facts before my Senate testimony in September 2002, I was disappointed to learn that no more than a few discussions had taken place on postwar matters. "Not a popular subject on the third floor [where Defense Department policy is decided by civilian leaders]," I was informed. When planning finally began, it was limited by the assumption that a U.S. invasion would be welcomed by the majority of Iraqis as a liberation. The strength of the Baath Party was underestimated,[4] as was the degree of Shiite factionalism, intrinsic Iraqi nationalism, the risks of covert engagement by Syria and Iran, and the fundamental risk that a largely Christian U.S. force would not be accepted by the people themselves, especially if it fought its way into the country.

Thus the entire postwar operation prepared by the Office of Humanitarian and Reconstruction Assistance under the leadership of retired Lieutenant General Jay Garner focused on the less critical tasks. But in fact, the primary problems were the restoration of order and a sense of legitimacy. These had to be dealt with before reconstruction could follow. And Jay Garner was left not only without the adequate communications, transportation, security, and staff resources to face these problems; he was also subordinated to U.S. military commanders in the region, rather than working directly for the president or secretary of defense.

The cumulative effect was to leave the mission isolated, with only the merest trace of UN authority and scrambling to persuade reluctant allies and friendly states to provide the police, troops,

translators, and civilian reconstruction assistance that could lessen
the risks to U.S. forces and spread out the burdens of reconstruction and nation-building. No program legitimized by international authority existed to sweep away the obsolete Iraqi laws or to
deploy peacekeepers to the provinces. Nor was there any mechanism, beyond direct appeal, to draw others into the mission. The
Bush administration simply failed to avail itself of the full range of
tools and support that could have been made available.

The irony is that some members of Congress, having carped
for years to the military about engagement in nation-building,
and complaining about "mission-creep" and "burden-sharing,"
were now going to have to support the American military as it
coped with this mission virtually alone, a mission that was (and
remains) far more difficult, dangerous, and open-ended than
any undertaken previously.

And this brings us to the third major criticism of the plan: In
attempting to retain full control, the Administration raised the
costs and risks of the mission by preventing our use of the full
array of tools available to win modern war. The Bush administration, thus far, has been unwilling to exploit the international
legitimacy and support from international institutions like the
United Nations and NATO. Rather than gain leverage via international legitimacy, the United States refused even through the
long summer of 2003 to cede political authority to the UN or
grant meaningful authority to any other international institu-
tion. Yet such legitimacy was critical if governments in Europe
were to provide forces and resources to assist postwar efforts.
And with greater international legitimacy, especially in Europe,
greater leverage could have been brought to bear on governments elsewhere. In the court of international opinion, the UN's
full authority carries substantial weight. All of this was poten-

tially available to the United States—if only our government had seen that it was necessary and decided to pursue it.

Operation Iraqi Freedom showed the need for greater multilateral planning and participation, especially for the postconflict phase. These are the perennial questions: Who is going to provide the police and ensure public security? On the basis of what authority? Will there be a judicial system, with lawyers, judges, and jails? Whose laws will govern? How will the nexus of organized crime, corruption, and quasi-governmental authority be handled? Asking the right questions, and creating appropriate solutions, is not a task for one power alone, not even a power as great as the United States. More than fifty years of post–World War II experience pointed toward the advantages of operating within the framework of alliances and multinational institutions wherever possible. In jettisoning these lessons for the convenience of a largely bilateral operation, the United States left itself substantially at risk legally, financially, and militarily. And no matter what the military language would say about "decisive operations," it was events on the ground in Iraq, after the big military operation succeeded in defeating Saddam's forces, that would in the long run be decisive.

As far as Secretary Rumsfeld's vision for transformation—a greater reliance on precision strikes and special forces, with a concomitant reduced reliance on large ground forces—operations in Iraq confirmed the wisdom of continuing to adapt in that direction—up to a point. But this was not a new vision by any means. The U.S. armed forces had been continuously transforming since they emerged from the Vietnam War in the mid-1970s. The forces that fought in 2003 were very much the product of five U.S. presidents and a sustained force development process that actually accelerated after the 1991 Gulf War.

After the 1991 war, the military establishment was determined to exploit the increasingly effective combination of precision strikes with the improved reconnaissance, surveillance, and acquisition provided by the E–8 JSTARS, overhead imagery, improved U–2 capabilities, and the potential of unmanned aerial vehicles. Step by step—from training and operational exercises, to strikes in Bosnia in 1995 and Iraq in 1998, to the continuing overflights of the no-fly zones in Iraq, to the seventy-eight-day Kosovo air campaign in 1999, to the 2001 war in Afghanistan against the Taliban—the armed forces practiced, analyzed, innovated, and improved. New equipment was introduced; officers who were captains and majors in the 1991 Gulf War were colonels and general officers twelve years later in Operation Iraqi Freedom. They not only learned from the overall efforts of the services—they brought their own lessons with them.

In 1996, the U.S. Joint Chiefs of Staff prepared, with the assistance of the service branches, the first real conceptual blueprint for joint war-fighting: *Joint Vision 2010*. This unclassified document explained the concepts of full-spectrum dominance, precision strikes, dominant maneuver, full-dimensional protection, and focused logistics, all of which were played out on the battlefield in Iraq. Insofar as there was a transformational vision, it certainly predated the change of administrations in 2001, and it had become a collective vision: taught in the services' schools, discussed in training and exercises, and incorporated into doctrine, materiel requirements, R&D, and procurement.

The vision heavily emphasized information dominance and precision strikes. As one senior officer explained it, "Imagine a box of enemy territory 200 kilometers wide and 200 kilometers deep; we should be able to detect every enemy target there, and to strike and kill any target we want." It was a vision compelling in its simplicity and clarity. It was an imperative and, in one way or another, was reflected in programs, budgets, congressional hearings, and even popular culture. The collective will behind the transformation was simply overpowering.

For the Special Operations Forces, a twenty-year effort toward legitimatization reached fruition in Iraq. Outcast after Vietnam, discredited by scandal and elitism despite incredible accomplishments and bravery, the SOF community worked step by step to break down the barriers of security and mystique that precluded their full integration into the battlefield fight. In Panama, in Desert Storm, on the hilltops overlooking Kosovo, in Afghanistan, and now inside Iraq, they brought elite skills, courage, and a very small "footprint" to battlefield success.

Thus, the irony is that the vision of transformation—a high-tech battlefield, viewed through an array of sensors, with battles fought and won by precision strikes and a slimmer ground component—which the Bush administration, and especially Donald Rumsfeld, have trumpeted, is largely a reality that they inherited when they took office in 2001.

Among those who insist that the transformation is not yet complete are those who cite the Army's need to improve its strategic deployability. After the difficulties in deployments to Kosovo in 1999, the Army committed itself to creating an interim structure of brigade-sized forces to be equipped with wheeled combat vehicles. This continues to be a work in progress. Others have cited a broader need to reform the larger, so-called clumsy division structure into something smaller and more maneuverable. But for the ground forces, many of the lessons learned are likely to be conservative in nature. For example, would we want to have fought without the M1A1 main battle tanks, which proved to be nearly invulnerable to Iraqi fire? Was there too much logistics forward when our forces were nearly out of fuel in the days before the advance to Baghdad? And despite all the criticism leveled against Army divisions over the years, those divisions proved themselves maneuverable, fully capable of fighting in brigade- and battalion-sized packages when necessary. Army transformation will need to move ahead—but with a clear-eyed view of the lessons from the 2003 campaign.

Of course, the broader defense transformation must be continued and made more robust: better sensors, hardened communications, longer ranges, faster missiles, smaller forward "footprint" of forces, better integration of service and special operations capabilities; and increasing capacity for network-centric operations. We can deploy hyperspectral imagery to see through camouflage; high-powered radars to detect underground targets; multicolored lasers to pass incredible amounts of communications; high-powered lasers to shoot down enemy missiles and provide close-in defense for aircraft and other force projection platforms; UAVs to orbit the battlefield and detect enemy electronics or enemy projectiles and calculate the transmitters or weapons locations nearly instantaneously—and so on. But the essence of the vision—the detection and destruction of enemy forces on a battlefield with minimum risk to U.S. forces—won't have changed.

The battlefield equation of dominating airpower grinding away at enemy forces—first their air forces, then air defense forces, and finally ground forces—is a winner, as long as the United States maintains its technological superiority over any foreseeable enemy. That is to say, we must maintain aerospace and information superiority. Our satellites must be guarded against a first-strike knockout blow, the Air Force must have the capacity to destroy any enemy air defense system, and communications must be secure against interruption and destruction.

Assuming a ten- to twenty-year horizon, U.S. military dominance is safe against anything but the emergence of a significant antisatellite system by a potential adversary or the secret installation of a network of hardened, largely underground, high-powered lasers able to destroy U.S. aircraft and missiles. These threats would enable another state to counter the U.S. transformation directly and to drive back warfare to its twentieth-century realities: larger forces and greater losses.

There are perhaps no more than a couple of states on the horizon that could envision developing such capabilities. China is one, but it is years away. States or groups that now want to fight the United States must do so asymmetrically—they must find new ways of undercutting the effectiveness of the U.S. way of war. Such potential adversaries will be drawing valuable lessons from the ongoing situation in Iraq.

But the experience in Iraq should warn us that both the plan and the transformation—or at least what we have heard of the Defense Department's vision of it—were incomplete, focusing only on "decisive operations," the "high-intensity" end of the spectrum of possible conflicts. In the mid-1990s, when we first committed *Joint Vision 2010* to paper, many were concerned about the need to balance the high-tempo, high-intensity vision of combat with the realities of what happens before and after conflict. This wasn't just Army or service-branch parochialism: The Army would most likely have to deal with these requirements and thus was the service most empowered to express concerns. We had seen repeatedly that the destruction of enemy forces was not itself sufficient to really "win" in most of the situations in which U.S. forces might find themselves. Defeating military forces was necessary to win the battle, but it was not sufficient to win the war.

We had witnessed the difficulties in fighting among the civilian population in Panama and in finding the elusive Panamanian president, Manuel Noriega; the problems of coping with the aftermath of refugees, instability, and prisoners of war after the Gulf War; the failure in Somalia, difficulties in Haiti, the challenges of peace operations in the Balkans. Each conflict involved a short, intense military encounter and a longer-term, less intense, but perhaps no less critical subsequent mission—and the armed forces would have to be trained, prepared, and equipped to handle these requirements.

There has been a very small constituency advocating the extension of the transformation debate in this manner. Institutionally, the Army has long resisted investments for and engagement in post-conflict and peace operations, instead of seizing upon such requirements as the kind of essential Army tasks that would justify continuing and perhaps increased resourcing and structure. Some of this relates to the existing United States Code (specifically Title 10), which prescribes the service roles and missions and mandates that the U.S. Army train, organize, and equip its forces for "sustained land combat."

Yet to be fair-minded, much of the reluctance can be traced to the military-industrial complex and the politics of organizational survival. Caught for years within a powerful vision of transformation that relegated its requirements to a lower priority, the Army, like the other services, hung its organizational existence on high-tech innovation and the creation of impressive, far-sighted procurement programs designed for high-intensity combat in the Middle East or Korea. These would be more likely to compete successfully for funding, given overall U.S. defense priorities, and, once funded, would pick up important backing from contractors and subcontractors in many congressional districts.

These imperatives were reinforced by the increasingly partisan atmosphere within Washington in the 1990s, during which the Republican-controlled Congress could be expected to react strongly against any preparations or resources directed at anything that might be seen as "nation-building." The truth was that the study, research, and preparation for postconflict operations was a political orphan. As George W. Bush, then the governor of Texas, stated during the 2000 presidential debates: "I don't think our troops ought to be used for what's called nation-building. I think that our troops ought to be used to fight and win war. I think our troops ought to be used to help overthrow a dictator ... when it's in our best interests."

Unfortunately, that is exactly how the mission was approached. In Operation Iraqi Freedom, the successes and failures of both the plan and military transformation were thus evident on the ground. In "decisive operations" the military itself had performed superbly, but in the larger planning requirements, and in the thinking about the true nature of modern war, the civilians themselves had misunderstood—perhaps it was all too easy to focus on the fighting, killing the enemy and destroying his forces. But every serious student of war recognizes that war is about attaining political objectives—that the military is just one among several means, including diplomacy, and that all must be mutually reinforcing.

The contrast with the controversial NATO campaign in Kosovo could not be more stark. There, international authority was invoked in a diplomatic effort to resolve the prospect of additional ethnic cleansing. For months the negotiations and planning continued apace. The UN was engaged early and continuously. NATO, rather than the U.S., bilaterally seized the problem. First, discussion about a threat, then the actual threats were used as leverage diplomacy. There was no preconceived timeline for action; indeed NATO went to extraordinary lengths to avoid having to act. Several countries leaders tried individually to broker a solution, and all this diplomacy did complicate the military planning.

Force was used as a last resort, and then only after post-operations planning and commitments had been made. The application of force was measured at the outset. And after seventy-eight days of bombing, and the threat of a ground invasion, Yugoslav president Slobodan Milosevic gave in to all of NATO's conditions: Some 1.5 million Kosovar Albanians were allowed to return to their homes, Serb forces withdrew, and a NATO-led force entered (with the United States providing only about one-fifth of that force). And today, Milosevic is standing trial for war crimes at The Hague, and Yugoslavia is an emerging democracy. No American soldiers, airmen, or Marines were killed in action during the campaign.

In Iraq by early June 2003, the signs of determined resistance on the ground were unmistakable. The United States was facing ambushes and sniping, especially north and west of Baghdad. These were areas through which the small U.S. forces on the ground had never fought—they simply arrived on scene in the midst of the postwar collapse of Saddam's government. Inside Baghdad, despite a gradual return to civil order, there remained isolated sniping, shooting, and sabotage. A shadowy Baathist movement calling itself The Return seemed to have emerged. The United States halted some redeployments of forces and undertook major military actions to reinforce threatened areas and attack the threat. As the overall ground commander stated, "This war isn't over yet." By September, more than sixty Americans had been killed and several hundred wounded in the continuing series of actions.

The campaign in Iraq had indeed succeeded in overthrowing Saddam's regime, but as of late August 2003, no weapons of mass destruction had been found. It was still likely that Saddam's regime had at least some programs in place to redevelop or enhance such weapons, especially the bio weapons, and perhaps even some weapons stocks, and that we just hadn't found them. But it was clear that new terrorist networks were being created or imported, in resistance to the American effort. Any democratic transformation of Iraq was therefore going to have to contend against a new terrorist threat, in addition to a multiplicity of cultural, political, regional and economic challenges. No one could believe at this point that such transformation would be easy, quick, or cheap. However, if a primary but unspoken purpose of the campaign was to demonstrate the skills and courage of the American armed forces, then surely it was a success. Now there should be no question about the courage of the American troops or their willingness to endure casualties—the Vietnam syndrome is largely behind us. It is time to lay aside the ghosts of past failures. Thirty years of dedicated effort have built a U.S. military without peer in its ability to defeat enemy forces on the battlefield. "Transformation," at least as it pertains to war-fighting, has largely occurred.

But power creates its own adversaries, and those seeking to contest American strength will seek methods that minimize the military advantages we have amassed. Much greater work remains to be done regarding the employment and implications of military force to enable the United States to achieve real success in promoting our values, security, and prosperity. All else being equal the region and the Iraqi people were all better off with Saddam gone. But the U.S. actions against old adversaries like Saddam have costs and consequences that may still leave us far short of our objectives of winning the war on terror—or, in themselves, may actually detract from our larger efforts.

CHAPTER 4

THE REAL WAR: TERRORISM

BY JULY 2003, many Americans still were questioning whether they were safe at home. The conquest of Iraq was complete, but there was growing appreciation that the occupation would require tens of thousands of troops, more than $100 billion, and several years to be successful. Are we any safer today than we were on September 10, 2001? That is the fundamental question for Americans concerning the global war on terror.

During 2002, worldwide incidents of terrorism fell by half, to the lowest number since the mid-1980s. By May 2003, about half of the most important identified members of Al Qaeda had been removed, either killed, captured, or detained. Among the kingpins were Khalid Sheikh Mohammed, the alleged operations chief; Abu Zubaydah; Abd al-Rahim al-Nashiri; Ramzi Binalshib; and operatives in Morocco, Pakistan, Belgium, Spain, Tunisia, Singapore, Indonesia, and an increasing number in Saudi Arabia, like Swift Sword. And in August 2003, the terrorist known as Hambali, allegedly the top Al Qaeda operative in Asia responsible for numerous terrorist acts there, including the Bali bombing that killed hundreds, was captured. All terrorists big and small were being hunted down, one by one. Their communications nets, as we knew them, were disintegrating. They were experiencing severe financial difficulties and cannot pay their supporters or provide for their families. We eroded their ability to carry out operations as they devote most of their energy to self-preservation. Despite threats and expectations, no terrorist activities struck Kuwait, Saudi Arabia, Western Europe, or the United States during the first month of war with Iraq.

Following the September 11 attacks on the World Trade Center and the Pentagon, a "floating coalition" of nations has been cooperating with the United States in the pursuit of terrorists, exchanging data, arresting suspects, and coordinating activities. The destruction of the Taliban regime in Afghanistan provided a flood of information—videotapes, computer disks, documents—that facilitated worldwide efforts to defeat Al Qaeda. This gave the U.S. efforts truly global reach.

Within the United States, passage of the USA Patriot Act by Congress shortly after September 11 facilitated the exchange of information between law enforcement and intelligence agencies and eased some of the operating restrictions that agencies had followed. Dozens of terrorist suspects have been arrested. Criminal trials are under way, and hundreds of foreigners living here illegally have been deported. Cooperation between the intelligence agencies is stronger than ever, with information coordination being strengthened through the creation of the Terrorist Threat Integration Center. The Department of Homeland Security, part of a sweeping governmental reorganization, was formed to organize comprehensive antiterrorist efforts, and a national strategy has been prepared. The United States has not been struck again, and Saddam Hussein has been removed from power in Baghdad.

Despite these considerable accomplishments, the global war on terror is far from over. Al Qaeda has retained its capacity to strike, as shown by the attacks in Riyadh on June 7, 2003, and previous strikes in Morocco, Bali, and Pakistan. Some of the Al Qaeda structure is presumably intact, with neither Osama bin Laden nor his deputy, the Egyptian doctor Al Zawahiri, taken out. For all the U.S. efforts, Al Qaeda clearly retains means of communications and funding. Of the several thousand persons arrested worldwide since September 11, many overseas have been released, and relatively few have been brought to trial. With Osama bin Laden still apparently alive and in charge, Al Qaeda is increasingly understood as a loosely affiliated, entrepreneurial association with potentially thousands of participants, some operating within so-called sleeper cells around the world. New threats were issued as late as the end of June 2003, and an attack on the Jordanian embassy in Baghdad that killed more than a dozen people bears the fingerprints of an Al Qaeda operation. In addition, the weapons of mass destruction in Iraq, the primary reason given to justify war there, had not been located as of September 2003.

Some Americans believe that success is merely a matter of time. That is a reasonable expectation, given our national military and economic supremacy and conviction that American values will ultimately win out. Our nation was staggered by the impact of September 11—almost 3,000 dead, billions of dollars in losses, declining travel and tourism, depressed investments, and a heightened sense of fear, especially on the East Coast. Yet we rebounded together with an enormous sense of determination, a spirit of political unity, and an outpouring of patriotic fervor. All these feelings were reinforced during the blackout of August 14, 2003, which turned out the lights across a large region of the United States; New Yorkers, rather than panicking, came together to demonstrate resilience as well as compassion toward fellow citizens.

But the analysis suggests that defeating terrorism is more difficult and far-reaching than we have assumed. Not only does the struggle continue; our success is far from assured. We may be advancing the ball down the field at will, running over our opponent's defenses, but winning the game is another matter altogether. Despite all our actions—despite our successes, courage, resourcefulness, and commitment—the overall approach has been seriously flawed. The roots of our mistakes date back decades, but especially following the attacks on 9/11 seriously misguided approaches, delays, and shortfalls have complicated and prolonged our struggle for security.

Modern terrorism made its appearance in the late nineteenth century as a form of political action directed against czarist Russia intended to force the government to institute repressive security measures, the theory went, and so lose the support of its citizens. Terrorist acts were incorporated into twentieth-century struggles against colonialism as weapons against the stronger occupying power. In communist-inspired wars of national liberation, terrorist murder and sabotage would be used in the early stages—so-called latent and incipient insurgency—to eliminate local leaders like mayors and teachers, thereby sowing fear, undermining authority, and provoking governmental repression. And terrorism became a means of struggle in the Middle East, as well, where the Palestinian organizations, among them Yassir Arafat's Palestine Liberation Organization, employed terror as a weapon of the weak to strike against Israel. As Israeli conventional military power grew during the 1960s and 1970s, terrorism enabled weaker Arab states to fight back—aiding and sometimes even directing anti-Israeli terrorist activities covertly—without risking defeat in conventional warfare.

Our allies in Western Europe were also under terrorist attack at various times. Germany and Italy suffered through the Red Army Faction and the Baader-Meinhof gang, Italy, the Red Brigades, Britain, the Irish Republican Army. Each group, it was believed, was receiving at least some support, directly or indirectly, from the Eastern bloc's intelligence agencies. In addition there were terrorist activities in France, Greece, Turkey, and Spain. The 1981 assassination attempt on Pope John Paul II, believed to have been coordinated by Bulgarian intelligence and the KGB, the Soviet intelligence agency, was perhaps the most dramatic expression of the threat. But our allies in Western Europe fought back domestically, through law enforcement, supplemented by military forces working at home.

U.S. perceptions were chiefly shaped by our Cold War rivalry with the Soviet Union and our strategic alignments in the Middle East, especially with Israel. Like Israelis, Americans looked first for state sponsors, because if we could deprive terrorists of bases, financing, and arms—all provided by states—we could drive them out of business, even if we couldn't penetrate their organizations or identify all their members. The Israelis, of course, went farther, developing detailed intelligence within terrorist organizations and on the ground within the region. We tended to work at the state level, building allies that would help us contain Soviet influence and expansionism, using others' intelligence and covert action capabilities while working to cut off support to terrorists.

Especially since the Yom Kippur War of October 1973, when

Israel was caught off-guard by coordinated Syrian-Egyptian attacks against the Golan Heights and across the Suez Canal, U.S. and Israeli military and security cooperation has been close. The United States has become the major supplier to Israel, selling aircraft and other top-line equipment, exchanging ideas on materiel and tactics, and providing extraordinary military and financial assistance. And to many in the national security communities during the 1980s, Israeli forces and procedures were examples worthy of study and replication. Israel was able to take older U.S. equipment and mount staggeringly effective operations, like the 1976 rescue of the Israeli hostages at Entebbe. Using U.S.-built F–15 fighters, Israel successfully conducted a long-distance, pinpoint raid that destroyed Iraq's nuclear capabilities in 1981 and, in 1982, swept the skies over Lebanon and Syria, taking down eighty-two Soviet-supplied Syrian aircraft in a series of actions without a single loss. It was a proxy fight of enormous Cold War significance, at a time when the United States was struggling to shake off the defeat in Vietnam and the tragic, flaming failure of the 1980 Iranian hostage rescue attempt. The terrorist attack on the Marine barracks in Beirut in 1983, which caused the deaths 241 American Marines, underscored U.S. unpreparedness to combat terrorism.

After the U.S. failure in Iran we began to develop an in-being U.S. special operations capability. We could be as effective as allies like Britain and Israel. Building on a strong tradition from World War II, special operations in Europe and Asia, including experiences in Vietnam, the United States soon created an effective, joint Special Operations Force that focused on hostage rescue as well as other forms of direct action and nation support abroad. But these capabilities, including much of the intelligence, were largely vested within the U.S. armed forces. The CIA, which might logically have conducted covert action, was hobbled by the aftermath of Vietnam, investigations into the intelligence community, and restrictions imposed in the aftermath. The CIA became habitually reliant on high-tech capability and the support of friendly foreign intelligence services. This would become one of the major U.S. weaknesses.

The end of the Cold War in 1991 spelled the end of much of the superpower rivalry in the Middle East. A simultaneous decline in terrorist actions, particularly events like airplane hijackings, caused some in the counterterrorist community to question their future. Without a superpower rivalry, and with the Oslo process promising an end to the long-standing conflict in the Middle East, was there still a terrorist threat? Indeed, all of U.S. national security policy seemed suddenly adrift, without a point of focus. Inside and outside the government, U.S. defense thinkers had difficulties formulating and orienting a new strategy to replace the Cold War strategy of containment.

Then, during the early 1990s, a witches' brew of Middle East and international groups emerged to shadow and threaten Americans. These threats were not motivated by the superpower rivalry or aided by communists behind the Iron Curtain. Nor were they clearly sponsored by any specific states. They fell outside the mold to which the United States had become accustomed. And they tended to draw upon the fundamentalist teachings of Islam, rather than the inspiration of class struggle, anticolonialism, or even anti-Zionism.

One of these was Al Qaeda, under the leadership of a wealthy Saudi named Osama bin Laden. Forged in the struggle against the Soviets in Afghanistan, and organized originally by the United States with Saudi funding and Pakistani support, this group moved from successes against the communist invaders to

new endeavors around the periphery of the former Soviet
Union, then into the Middle East and beyond. Based at one
point in Sudan, bin Laden fled to the safety of Afghanistan, built
an alliance with the Taliban regime there, cemented by money
and marriage, then established the hub of a substantial terrorist
network. The Al Qaeda leader had come to the attention of the
United States much earlier, of course, for our CIA operatives had
worked with him during the 1980s, but the severity of the threat
that he and his organization posed became clear only gradually.
In 1993, the World Trade Center was attacked by Islamic extremists associated with Al Qaeda.[1] And Al Qaeda became one of several different organizations seen as increasingly hostile to
Americans. It was only after the bombing of the Khobar Towers
barracks in Saudi Arabia in 1996, in which nineteen Americans
were killed, that we seemed to become clearly focused on the
specific threats directed against us.

And in facing this threat, we seemed to be breaking new
ground. Traditional Middle East power politics was less in play.
Iran remained hostile, and with Syria was still supporting terrorist efforts against Israel, but Al Qaeda was "supranational," drawing support from many sources. With its historic base along the
Afghan-Pakistan border, which we had helped to create in the
1980s, it moved within and drew support from residents, and
sometimes governments or elements of governments, of many
countries, including traditional U.S. allies like Pakistan and
Saudi Arabia. And Al Qaeda was not driven, as far as we could
determine then, by our old Cold War proxy rivals like Syria or
Libya, at least not directly. We needed new thinking, and we
needed to retarget our intelligence and adjust our means, for
with the Soviet Union out of the game, the technology-depend-
ent intelligence game was going to be different, and perhaps less

useful. In addition, some of our allies would have less relevant information to share.

Thus for some time we have had trouble understanding the real motivation of these new terrorist groups. They were not directed by states' policies by "deniable means," they were largely fundamentalist, acting against Western influences and power, and drawing most recruits from the anger, ignorance, and despair within "moderate" Arab regimes we supported.

The end of the Cold War and the breakup of the Soviet Union also forced us to think about new dangers such as the proliferation of weapons of mass destruction. There was widespread discussion about the dangers of Russian "loose nukes," as well as the possibility that skilled Soviet scientists, suddenly unemployed, would share their dangerous skills. Fissionable material or bioweapons might also find their way into the hands of terrorists or so-called rogue states like Iraq, Iran, and North Korea, which might still seek these weapons to threaten neighbors in the region.

Recognizing the potential danger, the United States launched a broad array of measures designed to track, stop, or limit weapons proliferation. The CIA established the Arms Control and Non-Proliferation Center, and the U.S. government tried with other nations to prevent states like Iraq, Iran, and North Korea from acquiring sensitive technologies and materiel. The Nunn-Lugar Act provided hundreds of millions of dollars to help identify and secure Soviet nuclear weapons, destroy launching systems, seal nuclear test tunnels, and hire scientists formerly employed in WMD programs. The Newly Independent States were persuaded to return their nuclear weapons to Russia and to destroy their missiles and launchers. Major U.S. purchases of highly enriched uranium from abroad removed fissile material to safe storage in the United States. International treaties and conventions were pushed to help establish inspections regimes to deal with the problem: the Missile Technology Control Regime; the Chemical Weapons Convention: the Biological Weapons Convention; and the Comprehensive [Nuclear] Test-Ban Treaty. These were the kind of quiet, broad preventive measures that only a great power like the United States could undertake.

But even with U.S. efforts, there were no guarantees of ultimate success: Scientists could be moved quietly across borders, key scientific and technological breakthroughs shipped out on a single computer disk, and lethal cargoes concealed in the expanding flow of world commerce. The opportunities for proliferation could be reduced, and the rate of proliferation could be slowed. But ultimately, despite all efforts, it seemed likely that at least some proliferation was unavoidable. Still, we hadn't come face to face with this reckoning. We had tried to draw a line in the sand on North Korean nuclear efforts in 1994, and we succeeded, at least temporarily, but we had long recognized that both Pakistan and India were undeclared nuclear states. And we knew that Iran was also striving for nuclear weapons.

Iraq stood as a special case—not a sophisticated terrorist threat, but the only one of several potential rogue-state proliferators that was legally bound under UN resolutions in 1991 to give up its WMD capabilities. Iraq had used chemical weapons in the 1980s war with Iran (of course, Iran possessed and used chemical weapons also), as well as in at least one action against its own people. After the Gulf War and into the late 1990s, Iraq was suspected to be seeking nuclear and biological weapons as well. The economic sanctions and UN inspections actually gave the United States a better grip in halting Iraqi weapons programs than, say, those in Iran or North Korea. Nor was there any substantial evidence that Iraq was connected to the more radical Islamists—indeed, though Saddam had tried to employ terrorism as a weapon during the Gulf War, he was a Baathist, a secular socialist considered an enemy by Islamic extremists.

In the United States, the U.S. foreign policy consensus that had broken down after the end of the Cold War was never regenerated. The Clinton administration preferred a multilateral approach in dealing with emerging regional instability in the Balkans, Somalia, and Haiti. But this also created an impression of hesitancy, delay, and, some said, weakness. As early as the end of the 1991 Gulf War, a group within the administration of George H. W. Bush had recognized that the collapse of the Soviet empire had opened the way for the United States to use its emerging militarily superiority much more freely.[2] By 1996, some members of this group recommended that Israel focus on removing Saddam Hussein from power in Iraq, both as an objective in its own right and to foil Syria's regional ambitions.[3] In 1998 Donald Rumsfeld and Paul Wolfowitz, among eighteen others, as part of the Project for a New American Century, wrote President Clinton asking him to "aim, above all, at the removal of Saddam Hussein's regime from power." They continued: "In the near term, this means a willingness to undertake military action as diplomacy is clearly failing."[4] But their case was based not on any specific Iraq-terrorist connections but rather on the fear that Saddam might acquire weapons of mass destruction and the means to deliver them, putting at risk "the safety of American troops in the region, of our friends and allies like Israel and the moderate Arab states, and a significant portion of the world's supply of oil." Taking down Saddam became a hobby-horse for many national security experts.

Thus instead of focusing on the terrorist threat, the Clinton administration felt the heat on U.S. policy toward Iraq, which had become the litmus test of the UN and U.S. leadership.

Nor was there much specific information that Saddam would be likely to team up with Al Qaeda to attack the United States with weapons of mass destruction. The reasoning was straightforward: Indeed Saddam had run an essentially secular state. He was a controlling personality, hardly likely to give destructive weapons to a group of Islamic extremists who were far beyond his control and viewed him and his state as an enemy. No hard evidence was ever distributed that linked Saddam to Al Qaeda. Terrorists were far more likely to gain access to WMD on the black market or by recruiting renegade scientists or other regimes, such as Iran, which had a long record of association with terrorism and possessed WMD capabilities, or North Korea, which was known to sell just about whatever military technology it owned.

North Korea was a unique problem. An angry, isolated regime, it had stooped to terrorism in the past and earned its hard currency from sales of internationally proscribed military technology. It had begun seeking nuclear weapons during the Cold War, and probably reprocessed nuclear fuel, seeking plutonium for nuclear weapons in the early 1990s. By late 1993, North Korea had pulled its first full load of spent uranium fuel from its five-megawatt reactor at Yongbyon. North Korea refused permission to inspectors from the International Atomic Energy Commission to examine nuclear waste materials to determine if plutonium had been extracted.

If the first fuel rods had been reprocessed, then theoretically North Korea might have had the materials for one or two nuclear bombs. The Clinton administration refused to accept a nuclearized North Korea, and prepared to build up U.S. forces for a possible preemptive strike. But war in Korea was averted thanks to bilateral U.S.–North Korean negotiations that provided the North with two lightwater nuclear reactors in exchange for abandoning its nuclear efforts. This agreement, known as the Framework Agreement, froze North Korean nuclear proliferation for several years.

Meanwhile, the radical Islamic threat against the United States continued to escalate, as groups like Egyptian Islamic Jihad merged with Al Qaeda. In February 1998 Osama bin Laden issued a *fatwa* against the United States, calling for a holy war and declaring every American a legitimate target. In August 1998 Al Qaeda truck bombs destroyed the U.S. embassies in Tanzania and Kenya.

Within the administration of Bill Clinton, a relatively detailed understanding of Al Qaeda had emerged by the late 1990s, including its overall aims, worldwide dispersion, and diverse financial support. The staging camps in Afghanistan were seen as its most exposed, vulnerable asset. And after bin Laden struck U.S. embassies in Tanzania and Kenya, the United States retaliated, with cruise missiles aimed at the Afghan camps, as well as a strike against the Al-Shifa pharmaceutical plant in Sudan that was suspected to be supporting WMD work and may have been financed by bin Laden. The missiles hit the camps, but apparently bin Laden had sufficient warning to escape. The pharmaceutical plant was destroyed, but evidence afterward failed to establish any conclusive link between the plant and WMD or bin Laden. The campaign against bin Laden largely dropped into the black world of covert plans and operations until 2001.

Throughout the Clinton administration, though, the efforts against the terrorist threat had been sharpened and increasingly energized. These approaches began as inherently defensive and limited in nature, emphasizing deterrence, defense, and protection of U.S. troops and facilities abroad first, then on actions against specific terrorist groups after they were implicated in attacks against Americans. This approach, as outlined in Presidential Directive 39, issued in 1995, was based on the concept of fighting terrorists primarily with legal and intelligence efforts.

From the perspective of the late 1990s, the implication was that terrorism would have to be confronted directly in the sort of semicovert, manpower-risking special forces and CIA campaign that the United States had never been particularly skilled at conducting; that going after terrorism effectively would require detailed, "targetable," predictive intelligence that was likely to be available only from inside sources; and that a campaign against terrorists would require a long and difficult series of problematic, publicly deniable measures. It seemed unlikely that we would be able to put a state "face" on terror: Afghanistan was playing a cagey game of talking and offering assistance, then failing to follow through; Iran had reportedly suspended terrorist aims against Americans in 1996. In Somalia there was no government to hold accountable. Yemen was slowly warming up to U.S. overtures. In addition, there were problems with U.S. allies in any prospective campaign: The Saudis were uncooperative, the Egyptians heavy-handed. Excessive reliance on Israeli intelligence and support in the Middle East ran the risk that the United States would undermine relations with friendly regimes, thereby conflicting with other foreign policy objectives. This had all the markings of a long and very difficult effort.

Nevertheless, active intelligence gathering on terrorist organizations was intensified, through both U.S. and foreign intelligence agencies. We saw a surge in terrorist threat warnings issued. Offensive operations were more challenging. A CIA-sponsored effort involving the use of Pakistani operatives to take out Osama bin Laden apparently was put in place after the attacks on the U.S. embassies in Africa but collapsed when Pakistan's civilian government was overthrown by General Pervez Musharraf. U.S. efforts would require support on the ground and involve a substantial "footprint," as well as significant risks. And without "actionable" intelligence, there was no point in repeating strikes by cruise missiles.

Then in October 2000 the USS *Cole* was struck by terrorists in the harbor at Aden. There was no instant retaliation. According to insiders, a decision was made not to repeat the futile cruise missile strikes against Afghan base camps but rather to prepare detailed, comprehensive plans to go after Osama bin Laden and his network. However, by the time the plans were completed, the Clinton administration was virtually out of office.

In retrospect, it was clear that more could have been done. And though planning was under way, its execution would fall to the next administration. Yet on September 11, 2001, the Bush administration had not yet approved a counterterrorist campaign.

In the aftermath of 9/11, a congressional investigation was begun; later, a presidential commission was chartered to investigate the whole failure. But regardless of the neglected warnings and unread memos, or even the failures between midlevel officers or within a specific agency, there was no doubt where the ultimate responsibility rested. This was a national security problem, and no matter how little or how much was done under President Clinton, the new Administration, after eight months in office, owned this problem. And the responsibility lay at the top, with the president himself as commander in chief.

From almost the very first moments after the 9/11 attacks, dealing with the problem of international terrorism seemed to become intertwined with older ideas, particularly the interest in finishing off Saddam Hussein. Barely five hours after the attack on the Pentagon, according to CBS News correspondent David Martin, Secretary of Defense Donald Rumsfeld was telling his aides "to start thinking about striking Iraq," even though there was at that point no evidence linking Iraq to the attacks.

According to CBS, a Pentagon aide's notes from that day has Rumsfeld asking for the "best info fast" to "judge whether good enough [to] hit 'SH' [Saddam Hussein] at same time, not only 'UBL' [Usama bin Laden]. The notes then quote Rumsfeld as demanding, ominously, that the administration's response "go massive ... sweep it all up, things related and not."[5] There remains no evidence linking Saddam and 9/11, in contrast to growing suspicions that other states, including Saudi Arabia, had many connections with the hijackers. And although Saddam and the 9/11 attacks were linked together in speeches and statements by many in the Bush administration, from the president on down, no one has ever proved that Saddam had anything to do with the one of the most costly security failures in U.S. history. Thus, at the very outset of the war on terror, some within the Bush administration sought to enlarge the problem and to use it as a means to address other issues. It was to become diversionary—searching for evidence to justify a campaign—and distracting—seeking to enlarge the problem rather than to focus on its essence.

But the administration wasn't alone in looking beyond the terrorists themselves. In the early hours and days after 9/11 many observers were suggesting that the attack was too complex and well-organized not to have had state sponsorship and speculating that Iraq must be behind it. Commenting that day as a military analyst on CNN, I received one of those calls, in this case from a Canadian, who closely followed events in the Middle East and suggested that I implicate Saddam. But he had no evidence to back up the idea of Iraqi involvement.[6]

Secretary Rumsfeld's alarming directives weren't merely angry initial reactions made in the heat of the moment. During the first days of post–9/11 meetings within the administration, attacking Iraq was apparently discussed, including at the weekend Camp David session where some elements of the overall strategy were first hammered out, though public accounts thus far do little to capture the intensity of the administration's early interest in finishing the fight against Saddam.[7]

Of course, the internal evidence pointed immediately to Al Qaeda, not Iraq, as the culprit. Al Qaeda had been operating from Afghanistan, which might be a much tougher target relative to Iraq. It is inland, mountainous, and remote. There was no existing OPLAN to work from in crafting a response. The Soviet Union tried, putting in around 100,000 troops, and failed to control Afghanistan. There was no time for the kind of start-from-scratch buildup that would take five or six months to mount an invasion force. And neither Pakistan nor the Central Asian states bordering Afghanistan were really suitable for staging a sizeable invasion force.

By contrast, attacking Iraq was in some ways a "natural fit," being consistent with or supportive of many of the foreign policy and political preferences of the administration. Action against Iraq would provide focus against a visible, defined, and widely disliked adversary. It followed the Cold War mind-set of assigning terrorists a state sponsor, a "face," that could be attacked. It was almost certain to be successful. It emphasized U.S. military strengths and built on a decade of preparation for a refight of the Gulf War. It tracked with earlier thoughts of some senior administration members emphasizing the window of opportunity for using U.S. military power to clean up the Middle East. And attacking Saddam was politically feasible—opinion polls right after 9/11 showed strong public belief that Saddam was somehow connected to terrorism. From this perspective, 9/11 was, some might have thought, a gift-wrapped opportunity, too good to pass up.

A few days after 9/11, I went through the Pentagon to double-check my commentary on CNN, visiting with the secretary and a number of old friends. The stress was intense. Not only was there high frustration and uncertainty about the future course of U.S. military actions against Al Qaeda; beyond that, some key military leaders within the Pentagon saw a misplaced emphasis in the internal discussions then under way. As one of the officers commented, "Sir, have you heard the latest joke making the rounds? That if Saddam didn't do it [i.e., 9/11], too bad, he should have, because we're going to get him anyway." And he continued, "We've never been very good at taking on terrorists, but one thing we can do is take down states, and there's a list of them they [i.e., the civilian leaders] want to take out." He was reaching out.

I looked at him as he spoke. We both knew that all this would distract us in the fight against Al Qaeda: first, the time demands on the military and intelligence leadership themselves—every hour spent planning operations against Saddam would have been used against Al Qaeda. Second, consider the intelligence collection systems: imagery, electronic intercepts, linguists, and agent networks surely would be more productive if not focused on collecting the tactical and targeting information against Saddam. Next consider the resources issue: Would we not have more financial resources to spend on military and homeland security needs if we were not simultaneously going after Iraq?

The overall administration strategy wasn't revealed at the time. In the public statements, shortly after 9/11, U.S. leaders defined the war against terrorism. As the president put it in his speech to a joint session of Congress on September 20, 2001, "Americans should not expect one battle but a lengthy campaign, unlike any we have ever seen. It may include dramatic strikes, visible on TV, and covert operations, secret even in success. We will starve terrorists of funding, turn them one against another, drive them from place to place until there is no refuge, no rest. And we will pursue nations that provide aid or safe haven to terrorism."

A week later Secretary of Defense Rumsfeld echoed the same themes, saying this war "will be a war like none other our nation has faced. Indeed, it is easier to describe what lies ahead by talking about what it is not rather than what it is." Rumsfeld continued: "This war will not be waged by a grand alliance united for the single purpose of defeating an axis of hostile powers. Instead, it will involve floating coalitions of countries.... This war will not necessarily be one in which we pore over military targets and mass forces to seize those targets. Instead, military force will likely be one of many tools we use to stop individuals, groups and countries that engage in terrorism.... This is not a war against an individual, a group, a religion, or a country. Rather, our opponent is a global network of terrorist organizations and their state sponsors."[8]

There was a clear offensive bias in the emergent strategy, with Rumsfeld explaining that "the best defense is a good offense"—better to strike the terrorists abroad than to try to defend ourselves at home. Still, the president announced in September that he would bring Pennsylvania governor Tom Ridge to Washington to lead the White House's new Office of Homeland Security. It was an anomalous position, in close proximity to the president and nominally responsible but lacking the kind of budget and personnel authorities that would enable the homeland security director actually to follow through on his mandate to ensure coordination and cooperation among various governmental elements. Everyone who had watched the so-called drug czar suffer through the previous two administrations doubted that such a position could be effective without real authority, no matter how personally competent and respected the governor was.

At the administration's request, Congress also passed far-reaching legislation known as the USA Patriot Act, designed to enable the United States to increase its ability to prosecute the war on terror at home. Essentially the Patriot Act reduced legal rights and protections for individuals in order to facilitate the war on terror: restrictions on wiretaps, information collection and sharing, detentions, deportations, and prosecutions for a broad array of crimes were reduced, along with constitutional protections. The bill passed both houses of Congress with very little public debate and no opportunity for the kind of extensive public review that such proposals typically warrant. Political dialogue had been stunned by the ferocity of the attacks—and the fear that more were planned.

To compound the fear and confusion, a scattering of individuals shortly after 9/11 became infected with anthrax, a well-known biological warfare agent. A Senate office building was contaminated and had to be evacuated to be disinfected. Florida, Connecticut, New York, New Jersey, Washington, D.C.—there was no specific focus to the infections—and it soon became clear that anthrax agents ("spores") were being spread through the mail system. Whatever the source—and the consensus soon emerged that it was domestic—the anthrax scare underscored the urgency for decisive action against terrorism.

Wisely the Bush administration didn't begin by attacking Iraq—instead, it found a "state sponsor" in the Taliban regime in Afghanistan. And despite initial misgivings from military planners about operations in Afghanistan, the United States attacked Afghanistan with the intent of destroying the Taliban regime. On October 9, 2001, then, the "different kind of war" began, with Tomahawk cruise missiles and B–2 stealth bomber strikes against Taliban and terrorist communications, headquarters, and other facilities in Afghanistan. In subsequent strikes B–52 and B–1 bombers deployed from the U.S.-British air base at Diego Garcia were also used, as were carrier-based aircraft.

The initial air campaign struck at only a few targets—a half-dozen airfields, as well as ammunition storage sites, some communications sites, and less than a dozen surface-to-air missile sites and air defense early warning radar sites. After a few days the inconclusiveness of these strikes was obvious to all observers. And there had been at least one apparent incident of unanticipated civilian casualties. The early effort looked tentative, timid, and ineffective.

Then, bit by bit, under Rumsfeld's strong hand, the campaign shifted to focus on Taliban forces themselves. Tank and truck parks were struck. Slowly and carefully, despite ferocious weather, small teams of American and British special forces were infiltrated. Within days the accuracy of the strikes improved. Forces under the Northern Alliance, a U.S. ally in this conflict, began to maneuver against Mazar-e-Sharif some 200 miles northwest of Kabul. The precision bombing directed by the Special Operations Forces put the Taliban in a deep dilemma: Staying deployed in defensive positions outside key cities made them easy targets for U.S. firepower, whereas retreating into the cities and built-up areas left them vulnerable to the latent hostility of a repressed populace. The Taliban had no answer for the combination of the Northern Alliance accompanied by U.S. special forces backed by precision strikes. First came the fall of Mazar-e-Sharif on November 9, 2001, followed by the siege of the Kunduz, the advance to Kabul, and within a few weeks the elimination of the Taliban regime in its home city of Kandahar.

It was a remarkably swift and surprising victory brilliantly conceived and executed: It involved about 300 people on the ground, several hundred carrier-based aircraft, long-range bombers, and less than 3,000 U.S. soldiers and Marines in nearby countries guarding a few air bases, plus the already established infrastructure in the Persian Gulf. Yes, the Taliban was extraordinarily weak militarily—but this operation showed that U.S. power had global reach, that the United States wasn't afraid to risk its manpower on the ground, and that the amazing U.S. military technology could also be effective against even remote, militarily backward forces.

By early December, the first major operation after the fall of the Taliban had begun, a slow, cautious advance into the mountainous terrain of Tora Bora, reputed to be the hideout and redoubt of Osama bin Laden. Allies from local Afghan tribes, accompanied by Special Operations Forces and supported by precision air strikes, drove away the enemy. In retrospect, this appears to have been a rear-guard operation by Al Qaeda; the local Afghan tribes probably allowed Osama bin Laden and most of his top associates to slip through the net.

In this case what had looked like clean strategic win against the Taliban became a missed opportunity that can be increasingly viewed as a partial failure. Like many missed chances and potential turning points, this one received only passing notice. Aside from the overall public impact, at home and abroad, of taking down the Taliban government in Afghanistan—and this was important—the strategic opportunity of the operation was to knock out Al Qaeda. The correct aim should have been to deliver a knockout blow against the terrorist network, not just against the supporting state. We missed our chance when enemy forces were able to scurry into the surroundings. Al Qaeda had been scattered—not destroyed. It might never again be so easily targetable.

From the early days after 9/11 some military leaders inside the Pentagon had expressed concern that substantial numbers of U.S. ground forces inside Afghanistan would be required to achieve success and that airpower alone, even with special forces backing up the local resistance, would ultimately be unsuccessful. As often happens, both sides in the ongoing discussions were half-right. Secretary of Defense Rumsfeld and his team were correct in assessing that airpower would be enormously effective and that the risks of inserting the special forces personnel were manageable. And President Bush correctly pushed for urgent, strong action. No unnecessary delays.

But the old Army thinkers were also correct in emphasizing the need for substantial forces—a U.S. Army division or two—to finish the work decisively. As it happened, the rapid collapse of the Taliban government found the United States unable to deploy the necessary additional forces in time. It was a strategic opportunity lost—and an eerie prelude to the bias in Pentagon planning that would lead to problems in stabilizing postconflict Iraq in 2003.

But this wasn't the only opportunity lost, or even the first failure of the campaign. That came at the international diplomatic level. Despite the worldwide outpouring of sympathy for the United States in the aftermath of 9/11, we squandered the chance to create a strong international coalition that could address the problems of terrorism comprehensively, beyond the limits of sheer U.S. military power, and also help share some of the enormous political, diplomatic, and economic burdens that the struggle would entail. At the outset, the United States gained United Nations legitimization for its efforts. The UN condemned the perpetrators, called on states to bring them to justice, and called on states to prevent and suppress terrorism, supporting efforts to cut off funds to some terrorist organizations.[9] But 9/11 was a crime against humanity. An international criminal tribunal could have been established to bring international pressure to bear.

NATO was also pushed aside, even though the United States is its leading member. At the urging of its secretary-general, NATO had declared that 9/11 constituted a situation that warranted invoking article 5 of the North Atlantic Treaty, that is, the attack against the United States constituted an attack against all member states of NATO. But, in essence, NATO was kept at arm's length, to be informed of U.S. decisions once they were made. A few NATO AWACS radar planes were sent to the United States to enable the alliance to contribute, but, as one high-ranking member of the administration told me, "No one is going to tell us where we can and cannot bomb." It was a surprisingly bitter moment for many of America's closest friends and allies— and a strategic error as well.

With the outpouring of pro-U.S. sentiment at the United Nations and around the world, the few weeks after 9/11 constituted a unique window through which the international community, international law, and the firm commitments of our NATO allies could have been fully engaged. But it was not to be.

Instead, as the United States sought to broaden its campaign beyond the purely military efforts in Afghanistan, it worked mostly bilaterally with other nations, exchanging information, deepening previous cooperation in identifying and tracking terrorists, and seeking to locate and cut off funding sources. This was the kind of detailed liaison work that the Federal Bureau of Investigation (FBI) and other federal agencies had increasingly moved toward during the 1990s and that, they insisted, was best handled bilaterally.

But the difficulties of moving in this manner became apparent almost immediately. In the first place, nations' laws differ, so the definitions and elements of proof regarding the crimes varied across borders. In addition, much of the overseas network wasn't involved in terrorism per se but rather in a variety of supporting logistics and communications work, the kinds of activities that are far more difficult to prosecute successfully. Legal procedures also dealt differently with electronic evidence, such as conversations overheard through wiretaps and radio intercepts. Such difficulties were compounded by the old issue of intelligence sharing, where the information received had come from "sensitive sources and methods," sometimes involving intelligence collection that a host government would object to.

A consequence was that some of the most obvious Al Qaeda suspects were merely detained, or detained and then released, especially in Germany and Spain, which had the more defined legal systems. Yet these were the very states, our allies, where the use of U.S. military capabilities was not an option, where Al Qaeda cells planned and staged operations against the United States and its citizens.

Here was a situation that cried out for work through a unified mechanism like NATO. States don't willingly assume expensive and difficult burdens, like changing laws and procedures, or deeply investigating their own citizens. Altruism and fellowship are not enough to bring other nations fully into the fight against terrorism. Rather, their international actions follow domestic political agendas. This is the genius of NATO, in particular, for it converts international issues into domestic political issues by requiring governments to take positions and defend them in front of electorates at home. The administration's resistance to fully engaging other states through NATO reflected a certain American "attitude," a lack of respect for the constitutional and political processes of other states, as well as an overestimation of American power.

The United States was left wrestling with a hundred governments bilaterally—an enormously difficult endeavor in something as complicated and sensitive as the war on terror. So what sounded easy at the top—a "floating coalition"—proved far more difficult to enact at the bottom of the government, where much of the heavy burden was being undertaken. And consequently, despite the thousands of Al Qaeda suspects detained worldwide, the network was (and remains) far from broken.

Meanwhile, in the homeland the first efforts had taken form within the intelligence and law enforcement communities to share information and track terrorists. Empowered by the Patriot Act and changes in FBI procedures, information sharing had begun in earnest, as tens of thousands of names of suspected terrorists were exchanged and databases searched and compared. The Department of Defense and the intelligence community teams formed cooperative efforts with those of the Department of Justice and the FBI. The work thus begun was, almost immediately, far more intensive and broad-ranging than any previously undertaken.

During the same time, the White House Office of Homeland

Security, responsible for leading the various governmental agencies, attempted to deal with broader issues. What was needed was a systemwide effort—at the federal, state, and local levels—not only to identify and detain potential terrorists but also to reduce the vulnerability of society to terrorist strikes and to strengthen our abilities to respond if hit. The first tasks were multiple: understand assets and capabilities available; survey ongoing efforts; assess vulnerabilities and priorities; develop a strategy and requirements. Homeland Security was a huge effort that would involve dozens of agencies, hundreds of thousands of people, and billions of dollars.

The early weeks of the Office of Homeland Security were spent, with borrowed staff and limited funding, organizing committees from the affected agencies, examining problems and policies, and proposing solutions. The magnitude of the issues seemed to demand an equally broad and complete staffing for every issue and action. An early effort by homeland security staff to gain control of some issues and associated resources was defeated within the Cabinet during preparations for the president's 2002 State of the Union address. In the meantime, efforts to establish demonstration projects and pilot efforts funded by emergency appropriations continued, though with few evident results.

Instead, many in the Bush administration seemed focused on the prospective move against Iraq. This was the old idea of "state sponsorship"—even though there was no evidence of Iraqi sponsorship of 9/11 whatsoever—and the opportunity to "roll it all up." I could imagine the arguments. War to unseat Saddam Hussein promised concrete, visible action. If any terrorists still thought that Americans were soft and reluctant to strike back, well, this would be the convincing blow. Success against an Iraq weakened by a decade of crippling economic sanctions seemed virtually guaranteed. And with the use of force in Iraq would come other opportunities such as breaking out of the decade-old "dual containment" policy in the Persian Gulf; pressuring other states in the region; and dealing with potential challenges to U.S. regional dominance in the oil-rich Persian Gulf before any significant threat to U.S. actions could arise.

As I went back through the Pentagon in November 2001, one of the senior military staff officers had time for a chat. Yes, we were still on track for going against Iraq, he said. But there was more. This was being discussed as part of a five-year campaign plan, he said, and there were a total of seven countries, beginning with Iraq, then Syria, Lebanon, Libya, Iran, Somalia, and Sudan. So, I thought, this is what they mean when they talk about "draining the swamp." It was further evidence of the Cold War approach: Terrorism must have a "state sponsor," and it would be much more effective to attack a state—with complete confidence that it can be taken down—than to chase after individuals, nebulous organizations, and shadowy associations.

He said it with reproach—with disbelief, almost—at the breadth of the vision. I moved the conversation away, for this was not something I wanted to hear. And it was not something I wanted to see moving forward, either.

What a mistake! I reflected—as though the terrorism were simply coming from these states. Well, that might be true for Iran, which still supported Hezbollah, and Syria, complicit in aiding Hamas and Hezbollah. But neither Hezbollah nor Hamas were targeting Americans. Why not build international power against Al Qaeda? But if we prioritized the threat against us from any state, surely Iran was at the top of the list, with ongoing chemical and biological warfare programs, clear nuclear aspirations, and an organized, global terrorist arm.

And what about the real sources of terrorists—U.S. allies in the region like Egypt, Pakistan, and Saudi Arabia? Wasn't it the repressive policies of the first, and the corruption and poverty of the second, that were generating many of the angry young men who became terrorists? And what of the radical ideology and direct funding spewing from Saudi Arabia? Wasn't that what was holding the radical Islamic movement together? What about our NATO allies, whose cities were being used as staging bases and planning headquarters? Why weren't we putting greater effort into broader preventive measures?

It seemed that we were being taken into a strategy more likely to make us the enemy—encouraging what could look like a "clash of civilizations"—not a good strategy for winning the war on terror. Taking down these seven states would do little to address directly the terrorists who attacked the United States, but it would probably make us the enemy of many governments in the region and to much of the Islamic world. The way to beat terrorists was to take away their popular support. Target their leaders individually, demonstrate their powerlessness, roll up the organizations from the bottom. I thought it would be better to drive them back into one or two states that had given them support, and then focus our efforts there. It would not be wise to go after a whole series of states first and risk dispersing terrorists among increasingly anti-American Islamic populations.

Additionally there was the issue of military feasibility. We could probably handle most of the standing armed forces in those states without difficulty, though Iran would be challenging—70 million people, much larger than Iraq, really difficult terrain. But what would happen after we got in? And what about the postwar plan? What would happen *after* we overran these countries? How would we govern and develop them, and why did we think we could do a better job of preventing terrorists operating there than the Israelis had done in the West Bank or in South Lebanon?

The Israelis had raced all the way to Beirut in a few days in June 1982—then faced a costly eighteen-year graduated withdrawal. And we had already grappled with Somalia and found it unpleasant—fighting women and children and irregular forces in cities was ugly and difficult.

If we wanted to go after states supporting terrorism, why not first go to the United Nations, present the evidence against Al Qaeda, set up a tribunal for prosecuting international terrorism? Why not develop resolutions that would give our counterterrorist efforts the greater force of international law and gain for us more powerful leverage against any state that might support terrorists, then use international law and backed by the evidence to rope in the always nuanced Europeans that still kept open trade with Iran and the others?

I left the Pentagon that afternoon deeply concerned. I hoped the officer was wrong, or that whoever was pushing this would amend his approach.

Military planning for Iraq apparently commenced during the fall of 2001, probably in accord with political direction coming from the highest levels of American government. By late December, presidential speechwriters were already tasked to "sum up in a sentence or two our best case for going after Iraq" in preparation for the president's State of the Union address.[10] And after the president delivered his 2002 State of the Union address, the policy was locked in concrete.

He stated that "our second goal is to prevent regimes that sponsor terror from threatening America or our friends and allies with weapons of mass destruction. Some of these regimes have been pretty quiet since September 11th. But we know their true nature." There were cursory mentions of North Korea and Iran, but the tough charges were directed against Iraq, which, in the president's words, continued to "flaunt its hostility toward America and to support terror ... plotted to develop anthrax and nerve gas, and nuclear weapons ... already used poison gas to murder thousands of its own citizens ... agreed to international inspection—then kicked out the inspectors ... a regime that has something to hide from the civilized world." The president continued: "States like these and their terrorist allies constitute an axis of evil, arming to threaten the peace of the world.... They could provide these arms to terrorists.... I will not stand by.... The United States will not permit the world's most dangerous regimes to threaten us with the world's most destructive weapons."

It was inevitable: We were going against Iraq.

The language in the State of the Union address itself was simplistic and bellicose. There were no obvious connections between Iraq, Iran, and North Korea—President Bush's "axis of evil"—beyond the suspicion that they each harbored ambitions to acquire weapons of mass destruction and the means to deliver them. Iraq and Iran were still at odds, technically still at war, more than a decade after their fighting had ended. North Korea, it was believed, would sell its military technology to virtually any buyer, but at the time there was no known supply arrangement with either Iraq or Iran. And while all had at one time or another used terrorist attacks as a tool of state policy, only Iran possessed an active and effective terrorist network through Hezbollah. And, in the President's speech, there was no evidence of any ties between Saddam's regime and Al Qaeda—any nexus seemed theoretical, a worst-case hypothesis.

In fact, in proliferation terms, by early 2002 both Iran and

North Korea were greater threats compared to Iraq. Iran had reportedly been actively pursuing nuclear weapons for several years and was believed to be using peaceful nuclear energy program as cover. And according to information later released by the Administration—though not until the congressional resolution authorizing the use of force against Iraq was passed—North Korea was actively pursuing a new uranium enrichment program that would eventually provide it with the necessary fissile material to produce nuclear weapons even if it never reprocessed the spent fuel rods frozen under the Framework Agreement in the mid-1990s.

The president's use of the term "evil" was also perplexing to many Europeans. At best, it evoked memories of former president Ronald Reagan's description of the Soviet Union as the "evil empire," a term that had raised European concerns at the time. Europeans, living on the same continent, were pragmatic, not ideological, in outlook, seeking survival, democracy, and prosperity. At worst, the "axis of evil" label seemed to foreshadow a religious-inspired campaign against sovereign states, something that could not only wreck international commerce but also pose domestic problems in European states with large Islamic populations.

Both the logic and language of the speech were a stretch. The international community struggled to make the connections between 9/11 and Iraq, and the U.S. determination to attack Iraq came to dominate much of the top-level dialogue between the United States and important allies around the world.

U.S. actions under way at Guantánamo Bay, Cuba, to receive Al Qaeda and Taliban detainees reinforced concerns about the United States. An old refugee holding area in the U.S. base, reactivated and prepared with small outdoor cells, was soon filled with more than 500 former Taliban and Al Qaeda fighters. Denied prisoner-of-war status, they were to be detained and interrogated. Some detainees, it seemed, might then be tried by "military tribunals" constituted to deny access to a civil court system that might provide inappropriate defendants' rights and thereby undercut the war on terror. The outcry from abroad was loud and sustained, as the fighters came from many different nations, including several U.S. allies. And the confinement policy itself was a continuing drain on scarce U.S. military police units.

Here the administration faced another dilemma of its own making. Having kept the UN and NATO out of the war, it had nowhere to turn for assistance in incarcerating suspected terrorists. It was good to have them confined, but the expense wasn't going to go away. In theory, the value of the information achieved through the interrogations would be high—but the costs of the internment were all too real.

And so, barely six months into the war on terror, the direction seemed set. The United States would strike, using its military superiority; it would enlarge the problem, using the strikes on 9/11 to address the larger Middle East concerns; it would attempt to make the strongest case possible in favor of its course, regardless of the nuances of the intelligence; and it would dissipate the huge outpouring of goodwill and sympathy it had received in September 2001 by going it largely alone, without support of a formal alliance or full support from the United Nations.

And just as the Bush administration suggested, it could last for years.

CHAPTER 5

FLAWED ARGUMENTS,
FLAWED STRATEGY

FOR THE MILITARY, the maneuvers in Afghanistan against the Taliban provided an invaluable rehearsal for the war to come in Iraq, but the real lessons would lie in the postconflict operations. By early 2002 the Taliban was on the run, out of power, but not destroyed. Al Qaeda, or some parts of it, remained in the region, sometimes in Pakistan, sometimes slipping back across the border in to eastern Afghanistan. They were still a potential threat.

The challenge for the Bush administration was to stabilize Afghanistan so that their real objective—Iraq—could be engaged. The administration had to take risks.

Afghanistan would be handled as an "economy of force" mission: "Here's all you get; now do the best you can." Control Kabul; pursue Al Qaeda remnants; strike at any resurgent Taliban activity; try to support reconstruction; but do not provide countrywide security. Despite the brave talk about new opportunities for the Afghan people, neither the resources nor the security forces were made available. The potential campaign against Iraq undercut follow-through in Afghanistan.

A government was patched together from disparate Afghan groups. Eventually a peacekeeping force was inserted into Kabul to help ensure the survival of the newly appointed Afghan leader, Hamid Karzai, amounting to a total of roughly 4,500 multinational (but no American) troops under British leadership. The International Security Assistance Force had no mandate to operate outside the capital. Nor, despite the pleas of President Karzai and the requests of UN Secretary-General Kofi Annan, was the force increased in size or made more capable.

In the meantime, while efforts to create an Afghan police force and train a national army were commencing, the United States pursued the remnants of Al Qaeda, which was assembling at this time in eastern Afghanistan and apparently preparing to resume offensive action against the coalition of Afghan tribes under President Karzai. The military action that came to be known as Operation Anaconda proved to be the largest U.S. ground operation of the Afghan war, involving three battalions of the 101st Airborne Division as well as hundreds of Afghan tribesmen accompanied by U.S. and British special forces.

The tactics deployed in Operation Anaconda reflected the new warfare. U.S. positions were planned on the high ground, from where troops could call in precision air strikes on any enemy forces attempting to flee their hideouts. American troops were to be the anvil. The Afghan tribes would probe and push and help develop the targets that the accompanying special forces would call in: They were to be the hammer. UAVs and manned aircraft with real-time TV links would monitor the battle, and precision strikes would destroy the enemy, position-by-position, until he surrendered.

The battle didn't begin as planned. At least one of the advancing Afghan columns was ambushed before it could move into its initial position. There was some bad weather, and intelligence information was imperfect: There were more Al Qaeda and Taliban than expected, and some were in or near the locations at which the American troops were set down by their helicopters. American soldiers were pinned under heavy fire—some forty were wounded during the first day of the battle. Apache attack helicopters as well as strike aircraft were brought into the fight. Two special forces transport helicopters were seriously hit and eight special forces troops were killed. After the first day, U.S. intelligence, firepower, and communications dominance assured a predictable outcome, and from that point on actions appeared to unfold as planned. Fifteen days later it was over—the Al Qaeda and Taliban remnants were dispersed. The only question was how many of the enemy had actually been killed.

But the operation had suffered from internal difficulties. After weeks of planning the Air Force, it seemed, was brought in only at the last minute. Then, relying on the routines that had worked previously, the Air Force was unable to deliver responsive fires in support of troops in contact on the ground. What followed were weeks of complaints, criticisms, and counter-charges, some of which reached the public and that in the end were addressed at the highest levels of the armed forces. Nevertheless, the operation had clearly demonstrated that American forces could handle the difficult terrain and tough fighting in Afghanistan. They could hang in a fight for days, without shelter or other creature comforts. They could sustain casualties and continue to fight. And they learned from each fight; afterward many would credit the lessons from this episode to have been responsible for significantly improved air support during Operation Iraqi Freedom in 2003.

Al Qaeda, too, learned its lessons. After Anaconda, the Taliban and Al Qaeda remnants broke down into smaller groups and continued to work along the border between Afghanistan and Pakistan. There were occasional actions against the U.S. detachments patrolling outside the capital. U.S. forces were periodically mortared and rocketed, and occasionally sniping and mining incidents occurred, even in and around Kabul. Thus the situation settled into an uneasy stability, with President Karzai in charge in Kabul while U.S. forces conducted a counterguerrilla campaign in southeastern Afghanistan, and regional warlords concentrated on rebuilding their own power.

As the Bush administration continued its planning and preparations for the looming conflict with Iraq, the ongoing conflict between Israel and the Palestinians suddenly exploded with Israeli military incursions into several West Bank Palestinian areas. Outrage and a wave of protests in the Arab world threatened to undo support for the U.S. operation being planned against Iraq. In March 2002 Vice President Dick Cheney flew into the region for a visit.

The Cheney trip looked to be a replay of his visit to Saudi Arabia and the Gulf states in August 1990 in which he had explained the threat posed by Saddam Hussein's invasion of Kuwait, rallied the loyal states, and helped gain the support that assured U.S. access to the region and Arab participation in the 1991 Gulf War. Twelve years later, reportedly, the results of this trip were far less satisfactory. Frustrations were high in the region; the Bush administration had done little to resolve the conflict between Israel and the Palestinians; and there was slim hope for obtaining broad Arab support for a U.S. military action against a fellow Arab leader while Israel seemed to attack Palestinian communities.

Meanwhile, at home, the first press leaks about systemic intelligence failures associated with 9/11 were threatening to raise political issues that might impact public confidence. It seemed that the FBI had been less than vigorous in following through with warnings from its own agents to check out flight schools for potential terrorists. And there was more to be uncovered as the classified congressional investigation into the intelligence failure associated with 9/11 moved forward.

In the spring and early summer of 2002, the business community, journalists, and policy analysts in Washington became increasingly aware of plans to attack Iraq. There were newspaper stories about Pentagon planning, with continuing discussion on TV talk and news shows. And in June 2002, while delivering the commencement speech at the United States Military Academy at West Point, President Bush invoked for the first time the idea that the United States had a right to preempt the actions of any country or group that might threaten us. This doctrine of preemption—taking action against others before they can harm—would be at the heart of the administration's case for attacking Iraq. In late July 2002, Senator Joseph Biden, then-chairman of the Senate Foreign Relations Committee, held hearings into the administration's plans for Iraq. The administration provided no witnesses.

In fact, the administration seemed determined not to confirm its intentions. In August, at his ranch in Crawford, Texas, the president questioned why people were challenging him on his Iraq policy. He was, he said, "a patient man." Defense Secretary Rumsfeld dismissed what he called the "frenzy" about planning for Iraq. But behind the scenes, work was continuing at a fast pace. And as Bush's chief of staff, Andrew Card, admitted one month later, "From a marketing point of view, you don't introduce new product in August."

The next step in the public affairs campaign was taken by Vice President Cheney during a speech in late August in which he described Saddam as a "mortal threat" to the United States, an enemy who could at some point "subject the United States or any other nation to nuclear blackmail." Vice President Cheney's remarks completed the administration's syllogism: If the terrorist strikes on the United States had employed weapons of mass destruction, they would have been even more deadly; the United States had the right to preemptively attack those who might threaten us, whether they were terrorists or rogue states; and Saddam, in seeking nuclear weapons, had become a mortal threat. In this syllogism, the nuclear piece was key, for it was the prospect of Iraqi nuclear weapons that justified preemption.

Here—and this was no doubt the thinking—was logic that everyone could understand, especially after 9/11. And regardless of whether or not Saddam was involved with those attacks—and no evidence had been produced to establish that he was—the lesson of 9/11 was so powerful that, it was suggested, no one would expect America to delay, to risk being struck first again.

But this syllogism, as it began to emerge, would require three additional factors to become compelling. First, evidence about Saddam's nuclear threat and its means of delivery would have to be established; second, there could be no alternatives to use of force; and third was the sense of urgency, or how soon we would have to act.

Meanwhile, the real irony of the war on terror, as it entered its second year, was this: Even without attacking Iraq—even as the administration had stopped discussing Osama bin Laden publicly—we seemed to be succeeding. Yes, we could have done better, invoking international law and using a formal alliance structure, yet we seemed to be making progress. There had been no attack on the U.S. homeland, and Al Qaeda's safe bases in Afghanistan had been destroyed. And after the Taliban regime had fallen, U.S. efforts against terrorism were continuing at home and abroad. Much of the important work was being done overseas by FBI agents in Pakistan and by the CIA in Yemen and other states in North Africa, Europe, and Southeast Asia, with U.S. and host-nation personnel teaming up. But these actions were largely unseen and unreportable. Instead the United States was already planning to go "over the top," using the terrorist attacks on 9/11 had suggested: seeking to use 9/11 as the basis for working another agenda, an agenda perhaps defined several years earlier, calling for the U.S. to use its military power to rearrange the Middle East, starting with Iraq.

By law, the U.S. president must present a national security strategy every four years (outlined officially in the document titled *The National Security Strategy of the United States of America*). The 2002 *National Security Strategy*, as it is known, is the definitive statement of U.S. national security policy, a durable document whose language is relied upon over the long term for making statements and resourcing decisions. Every word is fought over within administrations. In September 2002, the new U.S. strategy emerged formally, first glimpsed in the president's June 2002 speech at West Point and then confirmed with the official document published in September 2002. It was a broadly ambitious and ultimately ambiguous prescription for America's actions in the world—but its language and logic clearly pointed to the need for action against Iraq.

There was much in the 2002 *National Security Strategy* that was conventional and even idealistic, representing continuity of U.S. international relations from the Clinton administration and before. Sections elegantly discussed the need to champion aspirations for human dignity, speaking about nonnegotiable demands of human dignity, using foreign aid to promote a nonviolent struggle for democracy, and making the development of democratic institutions a key theme in our bilateral relations. Other sections dealt with the need to work with allies, prevent conflict, ignite a new era of economic growth through free markets and free trade, develop agendas for cooperative action with other major powers, and undertake a whole series of initiatives for strengthening the U.S. government's intelligence, diplomatic, and military capabilities.[1]

In describing the fight against international terrorism, the 2002 *National Security Strategy* recapitulated earlier administration statements, noting that the "struggle against global terrorism is different from any other war in our history, . . . fought on many fronts . . . over an extended period of time." First the U.S. will "disrupt and destroy terrorist organizations of global reach . . . and attack their leadership; command, control and communications; material support; and finances." The 2002 *Strategy* also called for working with allies, waging a war of ideas through public diplomacy, and, while restating the earlier theme that the best defense is a good offense, strengthening U.S. homeland security.

But the heart of the document was seen in the president's introduction, something he earlier described as the "crossroads of radicalism and technology." While citing the need for nonproliferation, the document placed a priority on "proactive" counterproliferation, explaining that the threat of weapons of mass destruction employed by hostile rogue states or terrorist groups is a newly understood threat and that "we cannot let our enemies strike first." This in turn required a new reliance on preemptive action—not in every case, but "proceed deliberately" and recognizing that "the United States cannot remain idle while dangers gather." As the president explained in the introduction, "America will act against such emerging threats before they are fully formed."

It was a bold statement, though to be sure American presidents have always had the option of striking preemptively—it is inherent in the right of self-defense. But this policy was more, much more. It became the centerpiece of U.S. national security strategy. Not only was it distinctively different in emphasis, it also pointed directly to the need to attack Iraq—precisely as the president had been hinting for months.

The 2002 *National Security Strategy* thus confirmed some of the worst preconceptions of U.S. methods and motives. It was a document fully grounded in U.S. interests as narrowly interpreted through national power. Headlines around the world cried out against a justification of U.S. unilateralism, warning that the United States had declared itself to be prosecutor, judge, and jury for what was acceptable in international security. International legitimacy and international law were not mentioned— though historically we have been among the most ardent proponents and beneficiaries. In the diplomatic hearts-and-minds struggle over the presumed war in Iraq, the publication of this doctrine was a heavy burden for allies and friends.

The publication of the 2002 *National Security Strategy* roughly coincided with the intensification of U.S. public diplomacy against Iraq that began in September 2002. On September 11, President Bush spoke in New York, and on September 12 he addressed the United Nations. The next week, the president met with congressional leaders. By September 24, the president was urging Congress to pass a congressional resolution. By October 2, the president and House leaders had agreed on an Iraq resolution, and by October 11 both the House and the Senate had voted to support U.S. action against Iraq.

Among the president's lines of argument in the speeches, two stand out as key: first, the implication that Saddam was connected to Al Qaeda; and second, the apparent imminent threat of a resurgent Iraqi nuclear program. The president said that Iraq and Al Qaeda had high-level contacts going back at least a decade. And he mentioned that in an alliance with terrorists, the Iraqis could provide chemical or biological weapons to terrorists that would allow Iraq to attack without leaving its own fingerprints. The president's efforts were backed by others, coordinated by the White House Iraq Group.[2] The rhetoric escalated, and skeptics were chastised with the warning: "We cannot wait for the final proof—the smoking gun—that could come in the form of a mushroom cloud." The intense, yearlong effort to prepare public opinion for war with Iraq, and to tie it closely to the war on terror, rested on fertile ground in the homeland.

Americans were predisposed to associate Saddam with terrorism and anti-American activities. In September 2001, just after the attacks, most of the public held Al Qaeda responsible, but according to Wirthlin polling data some 90 percent of Americans polled believed that Saddam promoted terrorism. November 2001 polling data showed that a majority of Americans believed that attacking Saddam would be "effective" or "very effective" in the war against terror. By August 2002, A CNN/Gallup poll found that 53 percent of Americans polled believed that Saddam was personally involved in the terrorist attacks of 9/11.

Yet the administration's case was weak. The Iraqi nuclear threat was postulated, not derived from new evidence, and based on largely discredited reports about attempted uranium ore purchases in Africa, a historical record of Iraqi interest in nuclear weapons dating from the 1970s, a hasty Gulf War nuclear program known to have been abandoned, and reports that Saddam had met with nuclear scientists for other purposes. The tie between Saddam and the 9/11 terrorists was also unproven, even after a year of effort by the Pentagon and the intelligence agencies. The links to Al Qaeda cited by the president in his October 7 speech were a decade old and had apparently not been followed up. There was no reliable evidence suggesting that Saddam was providing Al Qaeda any assistance in acquiring weapons of mass destruction. And the consensus of the U.S. intelligence community, as reported in a CIA letter to Senator Bob Graham in October 2002, was that the collusion between Al Qaeda and Iraq to attack the United States would be a "last chance," an "extreme step" undertaken only as a last resort if the United States was about to invade Iraq.[3] Thus, the administration had failed to establish the significance of the Iraqi threat.

Moreover, aside from frequent hints about covert efforts to overthrow Saddam from within, no alternatives to the use of force were attempted. Longer-term containment, accompanied by intrusive inspections, was dismissed without real discussion. The viability of inspections was consistently undercut by statements from leading administration officials who debunked them in principle as ineffective. Therefore, it mattered not whether Saddam complied with the UN Security Council Resolution or not—no compliance would ever have been adequate to assuage the Bush administration's concerns about his hidden capabilities.

Nor was any evidence presented of any imminent Iraqi threat to the United States or its allies. And imminence was the key.

The administration attempted to make its case—and to an

American public predisposed to accept it—but supporting facts weren't there. The United States could go to war in Iraq this time based on old evidence, fear, and intuition perhaps, but not as justifiable self-defense, even under a definition of preemption. Instead it was going to be a case of "preventive" war—an idea that the United States had consistently rejected for itself and condemned in others.

Within the United States, the case for war sold nevertheless through a combination of skilled public communication, fear, patriotism, and trust in the commander in chief. The Bush administration was on message, consistently delivering warnings and dropping hints. Secretary of State Colin Powell, who carried enormous credibility both at home and abroad, was the real arbiter. His authority silenced most of the retired military, like the retired General Norman Schwarzkopf and other moderates. There was trust in the president, too, as many Americans assumed that the administration simply knew more than it was sharing with Congress and with the public. And there was pressure directed against the doubters by an administration quick to identify and threaten critics.

The role of the media was especially perplexing. Despite repeated charges of "liberal bias" in the media, there was surprisingly little criticism of the war as the administration repeated its case, failed to achieve a second UN resolution, and hurried toward its self-imposed late-March deadline. Some suggested that the media's general acquiescence derived from a failure among Democratic leaders, badly split on the need for action against Iraq. Others cited media ownership by big business, especially the need for commercial media to capture audience share by not too closely questioning popular sentiments. Still others viewed the media as caught up in much the same emotions as everyone else—concerned with security, perplexed over the implications of Iraqi weapons and the threat of terrorism, and fearful of waiting too long to take action.

But several U.S. allies, as well as large parts of public opinion around the world, rejected much of this U.S. position. They questioned evidence, saw the failure to consider alternatives, and disputed the urgency of military action. Especially in the Arab world, where the threat from Saddam was seen more as a pretext for American hostility and aggressiveness, the U.S. interest in Iraq was often viewed, not surprisingly, in terms of oil and favoritism toward Israel.

The struggle at the United Nations that ensued over roughly five months was another heavy blow to the kind of strong international organizations, such as NATO, whose cooperation and resources are required if we are to fight terrorism effectively. In another strange irony, an administration that questioned the value of the UN wound up going to war with legal authorization from the UN but scant sympathy or support.

Aside from its actions against Iraq, the Bush administration was focused very narrowly on its efforts to combat terrorism: It went directly after the terrorists and their financing, ignoring most of the larger issues of prevention. Indeed, many of the 2002 *National Security Strategy*'s broadest precepts, UN resolutions, and other legal provisions have remained no more than ideas and opportunities, languishing for lack of funding and support, as well as those of a later publication, *The National Strategy for Combating Terrorism,* published in February 2003. Aid to international education and development faltered with funding cutbacks. The State Department remained starved of resources. Speaking out for democracy and human rights was hobbled by conflict with other foreign policy goals. Criticism of Russian activities in Chechnya was muted, perhaps to gain their support for the U.S. military presence in the "Stans." Efforts to work against corruption in developing countries have been complicated by the administration's rejection of elements of the proposed UN Convention Against Corruption.

Even the focus on the "crossroads of radicalism and technology" has been minimized, in that many of the most important programs to prevent the proliferation of weapons technologies from the former Soviet Union have stagnated. Funding for the Nunn-Lugar program, in particular, has remained essentially flat, despite largely unmet needs in chemical weapons destruction, tactical nuclear weapons control, and nuclear materials storage security. Despite claims of closer U.S.-Russian relations, Russia has refused to grant the United States access to four closed military biowarfare institutes. And perhaps most alarming, as the administration was concentrating on Iraq, North Korea—a country that certainly has sold almost every piece of military technology it has developed—was engaged in preparing and then reprocessing some of its spent uranium fuel rods, which would enable to North Koreans to extract fissile materials for as many as a half-dozen weapons.

In the more narrow set of actions directed specifically against terrorists, substantial results had been obtained. Testifying before Congress in March 2003, U.S. Attorney General John Ashcroft listed his accomplishments: hundreds and hundreds of suspected terrorists identified and tracked throughout the United States; human sources of intelligence doubled; alleged terrorist cells in Buffalo, Detroit, Seattle, and Portland broken up; more than 200 criminal charges brought, with more than 100 convictions and guilty pleas; almost 500 deportations linked to the September 11 investigation. Progress was also made in designating and dismantling the terrorist financial network, with more than seventy investigations and assets totaling $124 million being frozen around the world. And terrorist travel was disrupted: dozens of airport sweeps; more than 1,200 arrests for ID and document fraud; major alien-smuggling networks disrupted; and aliens and felons blocked from entering U.S. borders.[4]

But problems remained, both at home and abroad. Particularly in the area of immigration control, the existing systems were simply less than adequate. New systems for tracking foreign students, for example, were yet to be effectively implemented; a year after an embarrassing episode in which one of the dead 9/11 hijackers was given a visa extension, dozens of those on a watch list were nevertheless found to have been admitted to the United States.

There was also the critical question of civil liberties at risk under the Ashcroft methodology. This went to the heart of the war against terror: What would it mean to "win" in the struggle for freedom if we gave up our rights and liberties at home? Under the USA Patriot Act, passed by Congress in the aftermath of 9/11, restraints on wiretapping and privacy had been loosened. Such restraints had been imposed in the early 1970s when the chilling effect of governmental intrusion on civil society cast long shadows over American democracy. Provisions for secret, so-called sneak-and-peek, searches, as well as expanded access to a broad array of public records raised particular concerns. But thus far, the heaviest impact of the Patriot Act had, arguably, been on Muslims in the United States, many of immigrant origin, and on other groups of immigrants from Islamic states. Over the months, various nationalities were ordered to report for fingerprinting and identity confirmations; visa and naturalization problems were harshly handled, as individuals now suspected of terrorist affiliation could be held without charges and virtually incommunicado. As an infringement on rights, the Patriot Act should have been "sunsetted" annually, requiring extensive legislative and public review and reauthorization each year before any expansion of its provisions could be considered.

Great emphasis was placed on the value of the "floating coalition," but foreign governments' cooperation with the United States remained problematic. An operation to train Philippine soldiers and assist in the fight against terrorists was mounted in 2002. Operating in the Philippines required bucking the legacy of U.S. colonialism there, including the hard feelings accompanying the final U.S. withdrawal in the early 1990s. U.S. troops were not allowed into direct combat and were reduced to a supporting role. Still, the commitment of 600 U.S. special forces personnel and air support was effective in breaking up an Islamic terrorist and guerrilla movement that was holding captive two Americans. Continuing challenges remain in the southern Philippines, however, and sporadic terrorist bombings and other actions signaled the persistence of the threat there.

In Yemen, a pattern of rapprochement begun in the late 1990s has continued. U.S. elements were able to locate and strike one terrorist team and capture others operating or hiding in Yemen in 2002 and early 2003. But some terrorists detained by Yemen escaped, possibly with the assistance of authorities there.

Morocco, long associated with the United States and a valued partner in the continuing efforts to resolve the Arab-Israeli dispute, apparently worked with U.S. intelligence to break up a plot to strike warships transiting the Strait of Gibraltar and turned over other suspects. Jordan has long actively supported the United States, as have Egypt and many of the Gulf states.

Elsewhere, relationships are more ambiguous. Pakistan has

been the linchpin of U.S. actions in Afghanistan and has remained cooperative, turning over suspects, hosting U.S. counterterrorist activities, and working within limits to assist U.S. military actions in the region. In June 2003 Pakistan launched its largest military operation, involving some 70,000 troops, into the tribal areas to eliminate the Taliban and Al Qaeda remnants there. Yet Pakistan is a regime in danger, sparring internally with strong fundamentalist forces that have penetrated its security and intelligence networks. It is also host to a network of fundamentalist schools (*madrassas*), some of which radicalize and recruit youngsters for entrance into terrorist networks. Funded through Islamic charities and often espousing extreme views, *madrassas* will remain a key source of trouble in the years ahead. Thus far actions taken to reform their curricula or reduce their roles as recruitment centers have had little impact. Until this is done, Pakistan will remain inherently unstable, a source of the terrorist threat we face.

There were some presumed advantages in the U.S. action against Iraq, including the warning sent to other potential proliferators, sponsors, and traffickers in terrorism. Yet neither Syria nor Iran has mollified their policies—if anything Syria and Iran have been motivated to encourage resistance to American actions in postwar Iraq. North Korea, of course, took the message that it should develop nuclear weapons as soon as possible to provide a deterrence against potential U.S. action there. And in the summer of 2003 rumors continued to swirl that Iranians were hosting senior Al Qaeda members—despite Iran's occasional and teasing cooperation with the West.

Then there was the case of Saudi Arabia, from which the majority of the 9/11 hijackers had been recruited. The Saudis had always played a dual game, using the United States for their own security and financial purposes while espousing and funding Wahhabist Islam and its consistently anti-American outlook. Had the Saudis been really pressed to cooperate? Or was the risk of pressing them too great? Or had the administration simply believed that they were more cooperative than was in fact the case? But the Saudis were a problem.

In the United States, despite the absence of any attacks since 9/11, warnings continued regarding potential terrorist cells among us, as well as threats issued against us from abroad.[5] Given the estimates of 70,000–100,000 Al Qaeda-trained operatives around the world, the results to date indicate that much hard work has yet to be undertaken. At issue is whether any of this had been facilitated by waging war with Iraq or—as seemed more likely—whether the war would have jeopardized antiterrorist activities and supercharged anti-American sentiment in the Islamic world.

As might have been expected, the broad measures to reduce U.S. vulnerability and to strengthen U.S. capabilities at home suffered from our attention being diverted to Iraq. The Department of Homeland Security, whose formation was announced in June 2002, brought together many of the weakest and most difficult agencies in the government in a workforce of some 169,000 with a combined budget of $34 billion. Strategies were published and plans outlined, but the workload, combined with the reorganization, was enormous. Much of the leadership was heavily engaged in the problems of bureaucratic reorganization—hiring freezes, program and spending suspensions, synchronizing efforts.

An early priority ought to have been to establish standards, both for the government and for the private sector. Setting standards required hard choices that reflected priorities and philosophies. For example, in the summer of 2003, there was still no agreed list of all items of critical infrastructure in the United States or their priority of protection. Nor was there an agreement on what the standards of protection should be.

Security of the Internet and related technologies demonstrates a particular case of vulnerability, despite report after report warning of dangers. In fact, one of the great ironies is that the businesses most at risk are the least likely to admit failings for fear of further damaging business reputations. Hence, "the market" won't solve this problem; only government-directed standards are likely to be effective. This poses a continuing dilemma for an administration viscerally opposed to regulating business.

In the case of port security, media reports continue to detail the dangers of the millions of shipping containers that annually flowed into U.S. ports, but the risks are not yet under control. Even the additional $1 billion to be authorized in the FY 2004 federal budget was estimated to cover no more than half the existing needs in this area.

And even with so-called first responders—the local fire and police departments and hospitals that would be first on the scene during a major terrorist attack—shortages of equipment and capabilities are appalling. According to a June 2003 study by the Council on Foreign Relations, fire departments across the country had communications equipment for only half the firefighters on shift and breathing equipment for only a third; police departments were lacking the protective gear required to secure sites where WMD had been used; the numbers of police officers in midsized cities had fallen by 16 percent over just two years; public health labs lacked basic equipment; and most cities were unable to determine the nature of hazardous materials that emergency responders might be facing. And across the United States, interoperable emergency communications and significantly enhanced urban search-and-rescue capabilities were urgently needed.

Fixing the shortfalls would seem to require billions of dollars in additional resources—with some claiming the need for as much as an additional $103 billion over the next five years.[6] But the first requirement is for preparedness standards, yardsticks by which we can truly assess our needs. These standards simply have not been developed. Once developed, funding could be provided, along with a host of other systemic improvements, identified in various studies, that would strengthen our first responder community.

All of the resourcing needs were competing against other priorities, including the administration's tax cuts. Together with unanticipated shortfalls in revenues from a slowed economy, the budget was already generating a FY 2003 deficit estimated at more than $400 billion, with a deeper deficit predicted for the following year. The funds requested for homeland security, even though roughly double the pre–9/11 levels in some areas, were falling far short of requirements.

Meanwhile, by the summer of 2003 the situation in Afghanistan had deteriorated: There were persistent rumors about a resurgence of Taliban strength, and the evidence of Al Qaeda in Afghanistan was too great to deny. The U.S. forces there remained at about 10,000 troops, built around a corps-level forward command post. The International Security and Assistance Force had seen its leadership go from the British to Turkish, then to German-Dutch command, and finally to NATO. But the 5, 000-strong force remained locked in Kabul, providing security for President Karzai and his government. By the standards of the peacekeeping operation in Bosnia and Kosovo, these U.S. and international forces were less than one-tenth the size required.

In the provinces the warlords remained in charge. The first effort to kill the poppy crop largely failed, and civil works and assistance foundered due to chronic lack of security.[7] Paving the road from Kabul to Kandahar, the centerpiece of the reconstruction program, was delayed repeatedly, and overall international assistance levels were pitifully low; for efforts comparable to those in Bosnia and Kosovo, fifteen to twenty times more aid would be required. Visiting Kabul in May 2003, Secretary of Defense Rumsfeld declared that the major combat activity had ended and that the campaign would enter a new phase (of "stability and stabilization"), but the facts on the ground seemed to belie his optimism.

By June 2003, Hamid Karzai was appointing warlords to his cabinet in a last-ditch effort to co-opt them in order to avoid open civil warfare. International humanitarian workers were largely restricted to Kabul. U.S. and international forces continued to face resistance, both in the countryside and, with the explosion that killed four German peacekeepers in Kabul, in urban areas as well. By late June, an Al Qaeda spokesman proclaimed a new alliance between the Taliban, Al Qaeda, and an Afghan warlord, and leaflets were circulating in southeastern Afghanistan recruiting suicide bombers.[8] By mid-August Taliban and Al Qaeda forces had staged successful large-scale attacks against government, police, and military outposts.

Even though the Taliban regime has been driven from official power, they and other anti-Western elements remain a threat to the Afghan government. Operating in and out of the border regions of neighboring Pakistan, they continue to provide potential havens for terrorist recruiting and training operations. There is no end in sight to the U.S. obligations in this country, and by late August 2003 the administration was reportedly planning to double U.S. assistance to the nation-building effort there.

And in the months after the occupation of Baghdad in early April 2003, the cost of Operation Iraqi Freedom was becoming clearer. Fighting there continued, many had been wounded in the series of ambushes, shootings, and explosions that marked a low-level guerrilla war was under way. The U.S. troop level was expanded to over 140,000, with no immediate prospects for substantial withdrawals. The U.S. Army was about 60 percent committed to peacekeeping—force "rollover," without significant additional reserve call-ups, was impossible. The expenses were mounting, too. As Secretary Rumsfeld explained, the monthly "burn rate" for the Iraqi operation alone was close to $4 billion.[9] Annual costs of up to $100 billion certainly seemed possible, and the administration was having difficulty finding others to share the burden.

In his early September 2003 speech, the President asked for an additional $87 billion, reiterating the words of Deputy Defense Secretary Wolfowitz who proclaimed that the operation in Iraq "is the central battle in the war on terrorism." The administration was correct—that operation has indeed become the centerpiece—and that is the difficulty. Nothing could have more clearly captured the essence of what has gone wrong in the war on terror than the President's statement.

The strategy itself was flawed, out of balance: too much effort against Iraq, not enough against the terrorists themselves; North Korean proliferation neglected early on; war used as a preferred instrument rather than as a last resort; operated largely unilaterally rather than in concert with an alliance; insufficient attention to the pursuit of Al Qaeda in Pakistan and Saudi Arabia; and huge sums expended in military operations abroad that, if used directly in counterterror operations and in homeland security, could have contributed far more to U.S. security.

No matter how villainous Saddam Hussein, the war in Iraq had thus far failed to achieve its intended aims. Saddam, of course, is out of power. But no evidence thus far suggests any link between Saddam Hussein and the terrorists of Al Qaeda. The Iraqi nuclear program, much less any type of nuclear weapon, has not been found. Even in the area of chemical and biological weapons, where the intelligence agencies were certain that Saddam retained some capabilities, nothing significant has yet been uncovered, certainly not anything that would suggest an imminent and significant threat to the United States.

In fact, the Bush administration's focus on Iraq had thus far weakened our counterterrorist efforts, diverting attention, resources, and leadership, alienating allied supporters, and serving as a rallying point for anyone wishing harm to the United States and Americans. The failure to find the Iraqi WMD programs not only undermined the credibility of U.S. intelligence but also undercut other U.S. efforts to prevent WMD proliferation. Osama bin Laden and his followers could have hoped for nothing more than another U.S. attack on an Islamic state to rouse popular enthusiasm and recruit the next wave of terrorists. By mid-August 2003 the Saudi government reported that 3,000 of its citizens had "disappeared," apparently over the border to Iraq, drawn to the opportunity to engage the Americans at close range on their own ground.

Conversely, U.S. efforts against terrorists worldwide have been disruptive but thus far have yet to destroy the terrorists' abilities to recruit, fund, and prepare additional attacks. The failure to create a true multilateral antiterrorist alliance has undoubtedly delayed more effective efforts to harmonize laws, information, police work, and legal systems. And more generally, the administration's focus on "offense" is unbalanced, not only delaying protective measures at home but also reducing emphasis on eliminating the causes of terrorism and the risks of proliferation of weapons of mass destruction.

Unfortunately, we are now engaged and fully committed in the occupation of Iraq. And so, whether or not it was a wise operation, we will be not be made safer now by a withdrawal that leaves Iraq in chaos, allows the return of a Baathist regime, or permits the emergence of a radical Islamist state. Now, if possible, we must transform a successful military attack into victory by helping the Iraqi people to use this opportunity to establish representative government and the political and economic freedoms that can at least serve as an example to others throughout the region, as well as by demonstrating the awesome constructive power of U.S. values, ideas, and resources.

In the bright euphoria of the falling statue in Baghdad and the wishful thinking in Washington in early April, there was continuing talk of the New American Empire. It is an old idea, really, reborn of the pride and patriotism of a great American people humiliated for a generation by the legacy of Vietnam, hungry for the successes of the "Greatest Generation," and newly emboldened—and angered—by attacks on their homeland. But the idea of American Empire is a misunderstanding. It will not lead to success in Iraq, and it puts at risk much of what America already has—and what we could achieve in the future. Only the germ of the idea is correct: America, still the world's most powerful state, can be not only more secure but also a greater force for good. To achieve this, the old ideas of empire have to be replaced with a new strategic vision.

CHAPTER 6

BEYOND EMPIRE:
A NEW AMERICA

SOMEWHERE IN KUWAIT, March 21, 2003. The troops of the 101st Airborne Division were forming up, preparing to move. As they gathered the last of their gear onto the trucks that would carry them across the Kuwait border and into war with Iraq, they were a magnificent sight. All in uniform, taut and fit, talking quietly. Their weapons were slung over their shoulders, their rucksacks were hung neatly along the rails of the trucks. The scene reeked of training and discipline, the quiet professionalism of soldiers who have prepped for months and years, who know their moment is at hand.

No scene showed more clearly the achievements of the all-volunteer force or the distance our Army had come since the trying days of Vietnam.

In the days that followed, their performance lived up to their appearance and reputation. Driving through the dust and grit, fighting to clear the built-up areas of Najaf, Karbala, and Hilla, and later surging into the far north of Iraq to work with the Kurds, the 101st was a unit that burnished the reputation of the

American man-of-arms. They and the others with them fought with skill, with courage, and with compassion, using firepower in a controlled way to minimize civilian casualties and limit the destruction of local roads and buildings.

The powerful image of this American force sprang on the American public, and on the world scene, like the genie emerging from Aladdin's lamp—unexpected, almost magically powerful. Of course, the world knew that the Americans had the best technology, but this was real soldiering. The soldiers and Marines represented the values, the character, and the strength we sought in the aftermath of 9/11. They were not only the world's most powerful military force; they were also a powerful political message. As they carved their way through the desert landscape and overcame the scattered resistance, they seemed to signal a new American assertiveness, a willingness to risk power and lives for our beliefs. Their success could be seen by those who had taken us to war in moral terms: The triumph of "us" over "them" was the triumph of democracy over dictatorship, of free men over the enslaved, of good over evil.

Others saw the military operation differently. In the European press, it was an expression of pure power. In the Arab press, it brought invasion and destruction and the death of innocents. It was another example of the West imposing itself, in their eyes, even of the infidels striking the true believers.

But one perception was common: The U.S. military was so superior as to be virtually unchallengeable on the field of battle. Agile, fast-moving, hard-striking, air-land-sea capable, the U.S. armed forces would brook no serious rival. Perhaps not since the Roman Empire had a military force been so dominant over every possible opponent. And here, in this campaign in Iraq, the destruction and dismemberment of Iraq's army had been accomplished with vast U.S. capabilities left over. This was a military that could rewrite the boundaries of what force could achieve. This was an armed force that made a new kind of empire appear inevitable.

In the first place, there was an undeniable qualitative advantage—it wasn't just the technology, though that alone was breathtaking to much of the world. It was more the way the men and women in uniform handled themselves, under fire, and in front of the cameras. They were so capable, so competent, and at the same time so human. These were family men and women, fierce, determined, religious, patriotic—who had left behind devoted friends and loved ones but who carried with them the faith of their communities. For them the mission was not adventure but a noble calling, a cause larger than oneself or one's family, a purpose to live and die for. They were not just the new centurions, but a new kind of centurion, it seemed.

With so much power it was easy for some to believe that Iraq was but the first step. The troops were visible proof of the president's speech at West Point a few months before: "We must take the battle to the enemy. . . . In the world we have entered the only path to safety is the path of action." The action was not only in self-defense but also for a higher vision, as well, it seemed. As the president had explained in this speech, "Moral truth is the same in every culture, in every time, and in every place. . . . We are in conflict between good and evil." Thus he intended our action to be moral. And even more, constructive, for as the president had exhorted the cadets at Virginia Military Institute in April 2002: "America has a much greater purpose than just eliminating threats and containing resentment, because we believe in the dignity and value of every individual. America seeks hope and opportunity for all people in all cultures."

On the eve of conflict with Iraq the president was even more clear in the ultimate aims: "A liberated Iraq can show the power of freedom to transform that vital region.... Success in Iraq could also begin a new stage for Middle Eastern peace." The vision brought pride to America, reflecting self-confidence in our worth and the superiority of our values. But it all came down to success in Iraq: success not just in the military sense, after all, but in the larger vision, the vision the president had sketched in his speech at Virginia Military Institute, and in February the next year before the admiring crowd at the American Enterprise Institute. As the administration seemed to articulate its overall plan, this was to be a new America, reborn from adversity and threat, reaching out constructively to the world, liberating peoples, reforming a "vital region," enabling the emergence of a new, universal morality, and taking advantage of this unique window of American military dominance to secure into the foreseeable future our security and safety. It was to be a Pax Americana—and maybe even more—and it had been a dizzying journey from the presidential campaign aim of a "more humble" foreign policy.

But the quasi-imperial vision was never matched by the reality. For all its military prowess, the U.S. Army isn't an army of empire—at least not yet. In the first place the U.S. armed forces were built for war-fighting. Despite a heritage of frontier service in the American West, they conceived of themselves in Clausewitzian terms, of big battles and maximum violence. In World War I, General John J. Pershing had created, with help from the French and British, the modern, European-style U.S. Army with 1 million soldiers deployed in France. These were the big, square divisions—two brigades each composed of two regiments, mostly infantrymen and machine-gunners, plus the division artillery—altogether some 10,000 infantrymen per division. They occupied terrain, and they absorbed casualties.

In World War II, Korea, Vietnam, and afterward, the U.S. armed forces sought an enemy, focused on him, trained to beat him. It was a heroic image—the bayonet assault, the airborne jump, clearing the caves of Iwo Jima, the cliffs of Pointe du Hoc at Normandy. These were the forces of twentieth-century warfare, of mass armies and the battles of state against state. They targeted enemy forces—and after the fighting was done, they wanted to go home. They were citizens first, soldiers second.

Historically the Army had lacked staying power abroad. By the summer of 1919, a few months after the Armistice had ended World War I, Pershing's army was largely at home, being demobilized. After World War II the Army pulled quickly out of Germany and Japan, leaving behind smaller, constabulary-type forces, even in the face of a continuing military challenge from the Soviet Union. Throughout much of the Cold War, U.S. forces abroad were under constant fiscal and political pressures from home.

Casualties have always added to pressures to withdraw. Support for our operations in Vietnam ultimately foundered on the problem of U.S. casualties. And the better the communications and the deeper the media coverage, the greater the sensitivity, it seemed. U.S. operations in Somalia were ultimately defeated by the deaths of eighteen U.S. soldiers in a single incident. Successful peacekeeping in Bosnia and Kosovo was believed to be contingent on avoiding U.S. casualties altogether.

Moreover, the Army itself had changed since the glory days of the "Greatest Generation." As a consequence of Vietnam, it was now all-volunteer. As a result of new technology, which has transferred some of the fighting and destruction to airpower, it was smaller overall. Its units lack the infantry strength, the "boots on the ground" that had characterized the draftee armies of the two world wars and even Vietnam. In 2003, the active

Army stood at an authorization of less than 500,000—a little more than half the Cold War force and a paltry 5 percent of the World War II mobilization. Many troops were married. Despite their patriotism, these were men and women who would have to weigh the call of country against responsibilities to families. Simply recruiting and retaining sufficient soldiers is likely to be problematic. And supplementing the force with more than 100,000 volunteer reservists called to active duty added to the pressures to finish up overseas and return home as rapidly as possible.

In the summer of 2003, the troops committed to Iraq, around 140,000, plus another 15,000 or so in internationals, were a small force measured against the recent standards of peacekeeping. In Bosnia in 1996, more than 60,000 NATO and associated soldiers had enforced the cease-fire and peace agreement between the warring factions. The civilian population there was less than 4 million. In Kosovo, there were almost 40,000 peacekeepers in the province of slightly less than 2 million people, in an area roughly sixty-five miles square. Yet in Iraq, with a population more than ten times larger and an area some forty times greater than Kosovo, was the troop strength of 155,000 sufficient? Only four times larger than the requirement for minuscule Kosovo? This was a force that was largely mechanized and short on "ground-pounders." Outgoing Army Chief of Staff General Eric Shinseki's concerns expressed in February 2003, about the size of the force required—"several hundred thousand"—seemed prophetic.

Worse, the American force could not be rotated for refitting, retraining, and recuperation in a "steady-state" fashion. The Army was committed—at its peak the force in Iraq was more than half the deployable strength of the Army. In Afghanistan, South Korea, Kosovo, and Bosnia were other competing requirements. Any rotation of units would require mobilizing National Guard formations. No matter how great its courage and competence, this was a force whose size, focus, and all-volunteer nature argued against the likelihood that the president's grand vision would succeed.

Nor was it large enough to follow through on the most expansive visions of the early days in the war on terror, when there was a vision of "taking down states," sweeping across the Middle East, greeted by cheering throngs eager for freedom from oppression and the American way. Could it now handle a fight into Syria, and the subsequent duty there, or onward into Lebanon? Certainly, the airpower was adequate, and the ships could pivot offshore—for the airmen and the sailors, the further actions would be yet another extended deployment. But for the Army it was different—they were doing the dirty work, day after day, amid dangers and uncertainties.

The casualties and deployments struck at the heart of this force. Most of those serving had believed in the compatibility of their conflicting duties to family and to country. During the fighting, with the national sense of engagement, the patriotism, and sense of community involvement, it had seemed bearable. But occupation duty was another matter altogether. Even if the extended tour of duty was completed successfully, despite the heat and austerity, another call to arms might be awaiting immediately thereafter. There were already stories of helicopter pilots transferred directly from Afghanistan to Iraq. After returning home, there would be another rotation to a combat training center, more family separation, births and birthdays missed, children wailing and spouses unhappy. And every casualty struck a note of fear among the families waiting at home.

The U.S. Army that defeated Iraq was a great force, unique

really—but these weren't the Roman legions who marched into Brittany, across the Rhine, and conquered England, or the hardy Brits who sought fortune and fame along the Northwest Frontier in nineteenth-century India. No, this was an American force, unchallengeable in combat, fighting for their country's self-defense, committed to strike back at those who might be responsible for the terror of 9/11—even though no link between Iraq and the terrorists was ever established. But they were utterly void of any interest in the gains and glory of occupation duty far from home. It was not an Army of empire.

In the late summer of 2003, the U.S. Army itself was at risk, a victim of its success in forcing its way into Iraq. Unless there was a speedy reduction of the occupation requirements there, or a wholesale call-up of reserve forces, we might lose the essence of the Army that fought its way so valiantly into Iraq, a casualty not of enemy fire but of overcommitment and underresourcing, as its soldiers and officers simply opted out.

Nor was the public at home been ready to shoulder imperial challenges. 9/11, it's true, had provided the spark that could dispatch a mighty force for an unprecedented American action. But soon after the fall of Saddam's statues, the jingoism in the media was replaced by more routine dribs and drabs: unusual murder cases, sex charges against a sports icon, mounting concern about the continuing spate of losses associated with the early postwar period. The American people, it seemed, would rally for war. (As a British press lord had noted in an earlier century, "War not only supplied the news, it created the demand for it.") But when the uncertainty and excitement of the maneuvers and offensive actions stopped, public opinion turned away. The Americans wanted their troops home—and soon.

Despite all the evidence pointing to the unsuitability of the

Army to a long overseas deployment, no extra resources had been provided to prepare for a drawn-out campaign in Iraq. Moreover, other diplomatic levers had been neglected and international alternatives discarded. U.S. foreign policy had become dangerously dependent on its military. The armed forces were practically the only effective play in the U.S. repertoire. The armed forces had personnel, funding, and transportation. They could deliver relief supplies, organize training for armies and police, install communications and power, advise ministries of justice, health, and finance, build bridges, support election efforts, and inoculate and treat host populaces.

Other federal agencies were underresourced, lacked authority, had problems with congressional oversight, or were consumed in other problems and processes. We couldn't stretch the U.S. Border Patrol from the Interior Department, for example, to fix border problems in Bosnia; there were no great units of reserve police awaiting assignments overseas to conduct policing operations. And the Department of Commerce had not proved especially effective at bringing jobs to Haiti or Bosnia.

Nor were such problems within the primary missions of the armed forces. They often resented being asked to tackle these issues and brought a narrow, almost mechanical approach to the problems. For all their versatility, they lacked the knowledge, skills, staying power, and scale to really manage a large nation on a continuing basis. They were unable to create deep-rooted political development. They lacked the skills and experience to revise constitutions, rework property laws and criminal statutes, and work methodically to bore into the deepest aspects of the societies. Nor were the troops police officers; investigations and anticorruption efforts that would be essential in nation-building were largely beyond them.

The reliance on the U.S. military fed another unfortunate trait: the tendency toward unilateralism. In the conduct of military operations, the United States had no peer. No other nation could muster the intelligence capabilities, logistics, firepower, and deployable forces that the United States had. Almost every operation combined closely with allies meant an operation that was less efficient and perhaps more risky (and probably every good Army in history has felt that way). It had become too easy for the military to believe that this superiority would carry over into postconflict operations. After all, the United States had the transportation, communications, and logistics that no other power possessed.

The military was the go-to organization, of course, and its soldiers and leaders responded to an unpredicted situation with all the skills and capabilities in their command. But even its best efforts sometimes contributed to immediate difficulties with the Iraqi population. At the outset, coalition forces seemed to refuse—apparently on instructions—the postwar security mission that was their inherent responsibility. The secretary of defense even appeared to condone a certain amount of the initial looting and lawlessness in Baghdad. Then, when the military tried to impose security, it lacked sufficient forces to do the job—it simply couldn't occupy the breadth of the country, search for weapons of mass destruction, and simultaneously guard the many civil facilities and infrastructure needed for the successful transition to an Iraqi government. And when they went "onto the offense" by conducting sweeps and searching homes, they often lacked the interpreters to explain to families what they were doing and why—a classic mistake in a counter-guerrilla effort—offended local leaders, and swept up the innocent and uninvolved. Even straightforward self-defense, like returning fire if fired upon, would over time result in a growing number of casualties among innocent civilians, as well as mounting popular anger that would be difficult to assuage.

Policy blunders compounded the mistakes. Disbanding the Iraqi army—effectively adding 400,000 angry, armed men to the ranks of the unemployed—must rank as one of the least efficacious moves in recent U.S. peacekeeping operations. The policymakers underestimated the breadth of the Baathist organization, too. Rather than organizing the Baathist remnants and calling back the civil service, then having them renounce their allegiance, the policymakers managed to displace Baathists and then drive them underground, virtually ensuring continued opposition. And surely one of the largest missteps was failing to have readily available communications and broadcasting facilities that could have been flown in to gain information dominance among the civilian populace.

By late August, the U.S. mission appeared to be hanging in the balance. Certainly the United States had the preponderance of resources—if it could bring them to bear. And there was no opposing superpower to stoke the opposition, as we had done a generation earlier to the Soviets in Afghanistan. But the occupation had thus far failed to meet popular Iraqi expectations in restoring security and minimal economic standards; Saddam Hussein had evaded capture for months; Baathist elements were hostile; Al Qaeda and other Islamic fighters were entering the country; and a steady diet of daily sniping attacks, bombings, and ambushes were producing more casualties each week among the Americans. And even though the resistance was far from sufficient to defeat the U.S. military on the ground, it nevertheless cast a heavy shadow.

In effect the United States and Britain were engaged in a

three-level campaign. On the first level, mostly north and west of Baghdad, the Sunni Muslim Baathists and some Al Qaeda–affiliated elements were engaged in a low-level guerrilla war with the Americans, inflicting several American deaths per week. At the second level was the struggle to restore and rebuild the economy and civil society. Electric power was slowly being restored, petroleum production was increasing, gasoline lines were being reduced, and any number of U.S.-initiated civic actions, like food and water deliveries, were under way across the country to attempt to win the hearts and minds of the Iraqis. Despite the Iraqis' griping, the soldiers were proud of their work. U.S. efforts were generating momentum until the bombing of the Baghdad water main, followed by the catastrophic destruction of the UN headquarters (the UN was a major source for rebuilding the infrastructure), showed how hard the reconstruction task would be. At the third level, the Shiite Muslims themselves were organizing. They were the majority of the population, and their leaders were increasingly restless to end foreign domination and gain political power. It appeared to be only a matter of time before they would turn out the population in large numbers to ask the Americans to leave.

As of September 2003, the situation in Iraq was moving toward a turning point. Given the prospects for an indefinite, low-level conflict, the number of U.S. ground troops present was probably inadequate and certainly unsustainable without major reserve call-ups or tens of thousands of capable foreign troops. There were two ways out. First, the administration could hang tough, deny the significance of the problems, and hope that the combination of strong U.S. forces, growing Iraqi political participation, and an improving economic environment (as well as, possibly, bringing in UN forces without ceding any U.S. leadership authority) would combine to beat down the resistance within the next few months, then proceed to reduce forces enough to create the impression of progress sufficient to sustain public support. Or second the United States could backtrack on its resistance to UN presence, secure a new UN resolution, and move to internationalize the problem, enabling the United States to reduce forces by perhaps half or more on an earlier schedule.

The best hope seemed to lie in turning over political authorities to a selected Iraqi council as rapidly as possible, and securing a new UN mandate that would provide the legitimacy needed for other nations to send in troops and provide financial assistance, while at the same time seeking to create sufficient Iraqi security forces to relieve U.S. troops. And at last, in early September 2003, the President announced his intent to follow this approach.

Only if it moved adroitly to placate Iraqi opinion could the United States salvage its claims of wartime success, avoid further loss of prestige in the region, and enable the U.S. armed forces to prepare for another challenge. Such a maneuver might see the U.S. force drawn down from around 150,000 to perhaps 75,000 by summer 2004. But even then, the U.S. ground forces will have been stretched hard and will likely need several years and unanticipated additional resources to fully recover. So soon after the defeat of Iraq, the image of U.S. armed forces as the heart of a new empire—as a liberating force sweeping through the states of the Middle East, brushing aside terrorist-sponsoring regimes to create a new American empire of Western-style democracies—seems to be a fading vision. Achieving the transformation of the region seemed a generation away.

Still, others who were already aware of the worldwide dispersion of U.S. troops in small training and assistance packets had prepared a complementary idea. They saw American Empire already assured, managed and directed by elite teams of special forces personnel. Language-proficient, skilled in everything from martial arts to public relations, they could move into a small country and provide the traction on which all American power could be brought to bear. They looked at Central Asia, at Afghanistan, at occasional efforts in Africa, and saw how just a few well-trained and well-placed men could assure access and build relationships with local rulers. They could counsel, coach, or threaten—always obliquely—the leaders they advised. And when help was needed, they could use satellite-based communications to bring it in, dropping food and clothing or precision bombs, as the situation might require. With remarkable efficiency they could align that country or province with us.[1]

Of course, this wasn't a new vision—it was an old vision, recycled from the days of the Cold War. It was a vision not so much about enabling democratization as about helping rulers friendly to us retain or enlarge their power. It was far more effective at maintaining Pentagon "access" than promoting a broader, values-based agenda.

Much of the debate and some degree of the enthusiasm about American Empire seemed to misunderstand America's enormous power and its unique place in the world. The United States had come of age as a world power by the end of the nineteenth century. Surging in population and wealth, gorged on foreign, primarily British, capital in the decades after the Civil War, the United States by the turn of the century was the leading manufacturing power in the world, producing some 30 percent of the world's manufactured goods, compared to Britain's 19.5 percent and Germany's 16.6 percent. Ten years later, the U.S. share was up to 35 percent.[2] And the United States began to compete as an imperial power, seizing Spanish possessions in the Caribbean and Pacific, dismembering Colombia to create an independent Panama in order to build a canal across the isthmus, fighting a difficult counterguerrilla campaign in the Philippines to secure control of the archipelago, and mounting a "punitive expedition" across the U.S. border into Mexico in pursuit of the populist Mexican bandit leader Pancho Villa.

But here the American approach to classical empire ends, for deep within the American psyche has been the principle of national self-determination, and it has asserted itself again and again as America has charted its international course. Cuban independence was granted in 1902. Repeated U.S. military interventions in Central America and the Caribbean during the first third of the century never resulted in formal U.S. annexation or permanent legal control. Philippine independence was formally granted in 1946. And while Marxist critics might charge that the United States was following its capitalist interests into the subjugation of other peoples, this critique was altogether misplaced. The Americans tended, on the whole, to be "leavers," not colonizers. Interests in foreign adventures soon faded, military expeditions were scaled back and withdrawn, and local forces, sometimes with U.S. assistance and advice, took over. The United States had power and influence, yes, and its businesses sought to compete globally for gain, but it was not interested in legal control or classic empire.

And after World War II the United States moved strongly to resist the reimposition of colonialism in Asia and to encourage decolonization elsewhere. We denied substantial assistance as the French sought to regain full control of Indochina and pressured the Dutch out of Indonesia. We weighed in against the British and French when they invaded Gamal Abdul Nasser's Egypt in

1956 and encouraged the end of colonial regimes and white dominance in Africa, even mounting a strong economic campaign that eventually ended apartheid in South Africa.

Unlike classical colonial powers, we were large and rich in resources. We were much less dependent on foreign trade for our economic development. Rather than finding outlets abroad for surplus labor and capital, we benefited from enormous inflows of foreign direct investment during the railroad boom of the late nineteenth century. Giant companies that figured in the early enlargement of U.S. interests in the early twentieth century, like United Fruit, were eclipsed by the enormous growth of the industrial base at home. Our geography and economic development contributed to form a strong predisposition for isolationism in U.S. foreign policy.

In the aftermath of World War II, we fought off a return to historic isolationism, first under the leadership of President Harry Truman and Secretary of State George Marshall, then continuing through General Dwight Eisenhower's presidency. Throughout this period we were a net capital exporter and ran a trade surplus as well. Gradually, though, the United States began to run a trade deficit, even while its earnings from investments abroad exceeded its payments on foreign investments here. Today the United States runs both a trade deficit and a deficit on investment income. In addition, the value of U.S. assets owned by the rest of the world exceeds the values of foreign assets owned by Americans. That is, the United States is now in "net debtor" status to the rest of the world.

As a leading industrial power, the United States was caught up in the continuing evolution of world economic development. The value of the extractive industries—gold, diamonds, timber—that motivated earlier colonial efforts by other nations was declining in relative terms. While extractive industries, and the multinational companies that dominated them, continued to hang on in their market sectors, the terms of trade were shifting. New areas of wealth had emerged in travel, entertainment, medicine and pharmaceuticals, communications, and modern manufacturing. And for the most part, value in these areas was not achieved by dominating sources of supply but by access to markets and attracting foreign capital and talent.

The United States has continued to draw waves of immigrants hungry for freedom and economic opportunities—from the nineteenth-century waves of Germans, Irish, and Italians, into the early-twentieth-century East Europeans, to immigration from Puerto Rico, Mexico, Cuba, and then Central America as well as from the Middle East and South and Southeast Asia. During the 1990s the United States experienced the highest population growth rates of any developed country, largely as a result of more than 1 million immigrants per year. By 2001, the United States was home to more than 3 million Muslims of Middle Eastern and Asian origin.

In fact, the United States had been far too late entering the game to become a classic colonial power, exporting its manpower. The explosive population growth in the UK that had fueled British colonial expansion in the nineteenth century had enabled the United States to settle its own frontier. And by the twentieth century, the baby-boom generation notwithstanding, major segments of the U.S. population exhibited some of the same patterns of declining birthrates that were common across the developed world. Population growth in the Middle East, Latin America, Africa, and Asia turned upside down the population flows of classic colonialism, with the underdeveloped world flooding toward the center.

At the beginning of the twenty-first century the United States is the world's leading economy, accounting for about 20 percent of global output and, during the period 1995–2002, for about 40 percent of the world's economic growth. Over time the world economy has become disproportionately dependent on the U.S. growth engine, which has led to the strange result that the United States must consume more than it produces—while much of the rest of the world must produce more than it consumes. This is a benefit to other countries, which must find markets for their products, but it is most of all a benefit to ordinary Americans. No previous imperial power had done so well, either in creating wealth for itself, or in sharing the benefits with others.

And all of this was sustained not by a classical empire but rather by an interlocking web of international institutions and arrangements that protected and promoted American interests and shared the benefits, costs, and risks with others.

First were the security arrangements that emerged after World War II. Committed to deterring and containing the Soviet threat, Americans stationed hundreds of thousands of troops abroad—but much of the expense was borne by the recipient countries themselves, especially in Asia. And the majority of these troops were not scattered across the underdeveloped world but rather concentrated in the once-devastated (but now highly developed) lands of America's former enemies. Although Congress grumbled continually about costs, the truth was that such deployments provided important contributions to states that had become some of America's principal economic and commercial partners. Joined to them by formal alliances, the United States relieved these nations of some defense burdens, creating supranational interests in security but also providing a crucial U.S. voice in financial, political, and, ultimately, cultural matters.

Second, the United States exercised leverage through international institutions and arrangements. There were security treaties: the North Atlantic Treaty Organization for European allies, bilateral treaties with Japan and Korea. Acting with allies, the United States was able to distribute the financial, military, and political burdens of its global security interests. In Europe, NATO member states provided most of the ground manpower in the event of war. Independent French nuclear programs provided a backstop for Cold War NATO nuclear decisionmaking. Britain assisted in the Persian Gulf until the late 1960s. France and Belgium were active in Africa. And Japan not only developed surprisingly modern and effective self-defense capabilities; it paid a significant portion of the operating expenses of U.S. forces stationed there.

Then there were arrangements that facilitated American economic leadership like Bretton Woods, the International Monetary Fund, the World Bank, and later the regular meetings of leading economic powers that eventually became known as the Group of Eight (the G8). Central bankers frequently met, at least to share perspectives. The United States also used the General Agreement on Tariffs and Trade (known as GATT) to open new markets for U.S. goods, products, and services among competitors and was the leader in organizing the World Trade Organization to further regulate and expand international commerce. General agreements were led or accompanied by regional arrangements such as NAFTA—the North American Free Trade Agreement with Mexico and Canada.

The dollar became the principal world reserve currency. When the United States developed balance-of-payments problems in the early 1970s, it was able to shift the international financial system from fixed to floating exchange rates, enabling continued growth of U.S. consumer demand while other nations concentrated on export-led growth to feed the U.S. market. The oil shocks of 1973 and 1979 were absorbed, and then digested, yielding, more than twenty years later, a lower real price of oil, as well as a strong financial bond between the oil-producing and oil-consuming countries marked by reciprocal investments and exchanges of debt. The allure of an integrated U.S. market was so strong that during the 1980s and into the 1990s the United States was able to run enormous federal budget deficits financed by foreign investors and foreign governments' purchases of U.S. bonds. Foreign investments and financing allowed the United States to expand its economy—and to strengthen its military— without paying for all of it through taxes. It was partly a matter of economics: The United States was a safe place to invest, and the returns were good.

In short, American Empire was, to use a contemporary term, virtual. The United States was at the hub of a network of mutual interdependence, sometimes called "globalization." It was built on a foundation of international institutions created and heavily influenced—and some might say dominated—by the United States, reflecting the American values of free-market economics and popular democracy. Enabled by modern communications and transportation, this network facilitated access to markets and investment opportunities abroad, assisted the flow of talent and intellectual property, and fostered the spread of market forces and democratic processes around the world. The major beneficiary of all of this was the United States itself. This "globalization" was the New American Empire.

But it ran not only on the "hard power" of military security and economics but also on confidence and shared values. This confidence reflected collective judgments about broader U.S.

policies at home and abroad. In the aftermath of World War II the United States created a number of multinational institutions through which it communicated intent and expressed long-term strategies. And it was through and within these institutions, as well as by concrete actions, that values could be demonstrated and confidence sustained.

The United Nations served as a forum for communications, as well as for addressing some international issues less directly related to superpower competition. Its founding and overall design was driven by the United States, attempting to rectify the failures of the post-World War I international system that had led to World War II. Almost immediately, the emergence of the Cold War undercut hopes that the UN could serve as a means of collective security. But it did. Support organizations such as the UN Development Programme, the Food and Agricultural Organization, and UNESCO assumed extraordinary significance among populations in the less developed world. But even more important, the United Nations became the source of international law—for that was the status of UN Security Council resolutions. True, it was law without a real sovereign to enforce it—but the legitimacy it carried moved domestic politics in many countries.

The United States was an ardent user of this international system. There were treaties to regulate nuclear and chemical weapons, as well as treaties to regulate exploitation of the oceans and govern all manner of commercial activities. And many of the treaties were accompanied by the creation of monitoring and enforcement mechanisms and organizations, such as the International Atomic Energy Agency, the Organization for the Prohibition of Chemical Weapons, and others. The United States had representatives everywhere, ambassadors and delegates and officers detailed for periods of service. And, issue by issue, they worked to pursue and secure U.S. interests.

But the American way was not to rely on coercion and hard pressure but on persuasion and shared vision. To an unprecedented extent, the United States had been benign and magnanimous as a victor of World War II. Sharing international power through the United Nations system, deeply involved in assisting the reconstruction of the German, Japanese, and Korean economies, hosting foreign students and encouraging exchange programs, speaking out against the old colonial empires, receiving immigrants, the United States became an ideal, a model for nations around the world. American beliefs expressed in the Bill of Rights had inspired others around the world. We were palpably uninterested in classical empire—our motives were consistent with those of dozens of struggling freedom movements around the world. For our potential competitors in the developed world, the combination of U.S. economic strength and American ideals was difficult to oppose. For two-thirds of a century the United States was regularly viewed as the most admired nation in the world.

To an important degree, American power in the twentieth century was what Joseph Nye, dean of the John F. Kennedy School of Government at Harvard, calls "soft power," the power to persuade, based on American values. It gave us an influence far beyond the hard edge of traditional balance-of-power politics. It was based less on physically occupying countries and imposing laws and institutions, or even on wielding our enormous economic and military strength, as old colonialism might have been, and more on leading by example, on transparency, and outreach.

Throughout the Cold War, the United States was challenged

to maintain its high principles abroad in the face of the Soviet threat. Some mistakes were made, and the United States gradually lost some of its moral edge, creating adversaries and doubters. Worried about potential Soviet encroachments into the Middle East, the United States deposed an Iranian leader and replaced him with an unpopular shah. Siding against a Soviet-oriented India, the United States distanced itself from the world's largest democracy. Fearing a Marxist takeover of Chile, the United States backed Chilean military action to throw out the democratically elected Marxist leader, Salvador Allende. In Central America the United States fought for almost a decade against Marxist-inspired governments and guerrillas using CIA and special forces personnel, as well as local movements—a struggle that succeeded, but at enormous human costs, with additional human rights violations and illegal government activities. A semantic distinction was often made between totalitarian regimes, which we opposed, and regimes that were merely authoritarian, which could serve U.S. interests—but it was an uncomfortable distinction, never fully accepted across the American political spectrum.

The end of the Cold War removed the source of these contradictions in U.S. policy. The United States was freed not only to expound principles but also to more directly encourage those that aligned with our values. And, conversely, the United States was less constrained in condemning states that habitually violated human rights. This new strain of idealism in U.S. foreign policy was reinforced during the 1990s by U.S. actions to depose a Haitian junta blocking democratic government there, and by the U.S. military peace operations in the Balkans, Latin America, Africa, and Asia.

But 2001 marked a profound departure in U.S. foreign policy.

Coming to power in a disputed election, the Bush administration acted unambiguously to put a more unilateralist, balance-of-power stamp on U.S. foreign policy. The United States withdrew from international efforts to address global warming, the Kyoto Treaty. The administration made clear that it would proceed with national missile defense regardless of the U.S.-Soviet Anti-Ballistic Missile Treaty, the South Korea–North Korea dialogue was essentially rejected, and a new proposal to focus the UN on tightening sanctions against Iraq was dropped. Even before 9/11 it was clear that U.S. foreign policy had changed tack.

Responding to the events of 9/11, the Bush administration abandoned its "more humble foreign policy." Overnight, U.S. foreign policy became not only unilateralist but moralistic, intensely patriotic, and assertive, planning military action against Iraq and perhaps other states in the Middle East, and intimating the New American Empire. Impacting an American public reeling under the shock of 9/11, the message played powerfully at home, dampening concerns about rising unemployment and the soaring budget deficit. And the risks were discounted. No matter that the aggressive unilateralism would hamper counterterror efforts, turn upside down five decades of work to establish an international system to help reduce conflict, undercut the alliance that had maintained security for half a century in Europe, and shake relations critical to maintaining the web of interdependence central to American prosperity. By September 2003, U.S. forces were in Iraq—deeply committed, without as yet a clear strategy either to salvage success or to exit, continuing discussion about possibly expanding the area of military action to include Syria and perhaps other states in the region.

But this shift—rather than promoting the emergence of the New American Empire—put all that we gained with "soft power" and the virtual American Empire at risk. The new approach has produced an outburst of worldwide anti-American sentiment. Opinion polls in many nations showed substantial numbers who thought that "bin Laden was more likely to do the right thing than Bush." These were concerns not about American values or how we lived but about how America acted abroad. Because such concerns reflect judgments about American actions, they would not be countered easily by advertising and public relations techniques. And they would affect the support the United States receive abroad.

Individually, some governments, especially democratic governments who must listen to the opinions of voters, would simply find it more difficult to comply with American wishes. Turkey, for example, refused to support the passage of U.S. troops in the war on Iraq and as of early September had yet to take up U.S. requests to assist with a peacekeeping force. India declined the request to participate because the mission was not under UN control. Germany and France also declined.

These are only the latest signs of nations beginning to define their own national interests by refusing unilateralist U.S. "leadership." What was emerging was more subtle, a more or less informal constellation of interests among several states, including both allies and former adversaries, to frustrate and complicate U.S. policies and objectives that were increasingly seen at odds with their own interests. Fundamentally, this risked unraveling the political and economic structures of interdependence that have proved so favorable to the United States. In the narrowest sense, if foreigners should lose confidence in U.S. leadership and reject the implicit understandings and economic alignments that have led them—especially the central banks of China, Taiwan, and Japan—to accumulate dollar holdings, they could quickly diversify out of dollar assets, triggering a sharp decline in the dollar's values and significantly impacting our economy. Somewhere in the rising U.S. budget deficits, the balance-of-payments current accounts deficits, and the growing resentment of the United States abroad, there may be a "tipping point," as yet undetermined. It could be triggered by geopolitical failure on the Korean Peninsula or in South Asia, a severe oil shock derived from simultaneous domestic failures in several producer countries, or simply the rapid enlargement of more attractive investment opportunities in China and India, and greater confidence in the Euro, sufficient to choke down the continuing influx of foreign financing. Or we could simply suffer a continuing gradual erosion of U.S. influence.

If leadership is defined as "persuading the other fellow to want to do what you want him to do," as Eisenhower put it, then American leadership was failing. We simply weren't persuading others to align with our interests—we were coercing and pressuring. Without a change in our approach, we were heading toward a less powerful and relevant America, regardless of the numbers of stealth bombers we deployed or countries we "accessed." If this path led to American Empire in the sense of more countries occupied by U.S. troops, it would lead to a poorer, more isolated, and less secure America.

But in leading America's response to the catastrophe of 9/11, the administration has enjoyed its greatest popularity in association with the men and women of the armed forces and when wielding the sword of American military power. This was no accidental occurrence. The emergence of a unilateralist strain in U.S. foreign policy had deep roots at home.

For more than thirty years, many Americans had seen their values under assault from affirmative action, from the rise of

feminism and the sexual revolution, from an American government that has seemed increasingly intrusive and inept in issues
like enforced school busing, and that appeared to coddle crimi-
nals while increasing demands on ordinary working people.
Household standards of living have barely been maintained
despite wholesale increases in two-income households. Congressional Budget Office data collected in 2001 showed, for example,
that the average after-tax household real income of the middle
fifth of Americans had gone from $31,700 in 1979 to $33, 200 in
1997. (During this same period the top 1 percent of American
households saw their family income rise during the same period
from an average of $256,400 to $644,300.[3])

Much of America had been engaged in a long-running "culture war" to fight back. It began in the reaction against the vio-
lent, protest-marred 1968 Democratic National Convention in
Chicago. It gained strength in the resonance that greeted Vice
President Spiro Agnew's 1970 attacks on the "nattering nabobs of
negativism." This was the "Silent Majority" of 1972, and later the
"Reagan Democrats." It was seen in the growing power of born-
again Christianity, the right-to-life movement, home-schooling,
and the rise of the National Rifle Association. Issues like abor-
tion rights, gun control, gay marriage, and the marriage penalty
became touchstones for a middle class under stress and seeking
to defend itself.

The conflict also spilled over into foreign affairs and was fueled
by shame at the withdrawal from Vietnam, controversy over the
Panama Canal treaties, and anger at American impotence during
the Iran hostage crisis. The culture war at home merged with a
fierce nostalgia for visible battlefield success abroad.

The American political system caught and reflected the public's views. Ronald Reagan called it "morning in America," a new

hope—but it was expressed most effectively in a boldly assertive foreign policy and in unapologetically patriotic policies that challenged the Soviet "evil empire" with the 1983 Strategic Defense Initiative ("Star Wars"), invaded the Caribbean island of Grenada, struck out in a 1986 bombing raid on Libya's terrorist-supporting leader Muammar Qaddafi, and called on Soviet leader Mikhail Gorbachev to "tear down this wall" in Berlin. Taking over from Reagan, President George H. W. Bush then rode the same crest of patriotism in the 1991 Gulf War—though severe economic distress, a third-party presidential candidate, and a charismatic young Democrat cost him a second term in office.

Transforming frustration at home into action abroad has emerged as a pattern in democracies under stress. It had happened in ancient Rome, in the Netherlands, and in Britain. And like most distractions, it provided false reassurance and was followed by damaging consequences. In Rome, a republic was transformed into an empire, the proud citizenry reduced to a landless plebian class. In the Netherlands and Britain, the "venting" led to jingoism and war, and war to greater financial burdens that essentially undercut the remaining foundations of prosperity.

In the aftermath of 9/11, when the Bush administration abandoned its "more humble" foreign policy, it also tapped the same source of power as its predecessors—now reinforced by real fear and determination.

But the administration's approach not only risked America's virtual empire abroad but also undercut America's hard power as well, for we can be no stronger abroad than we are at home. Pushing through substantial tax cuts—costing hundreds of billions of dollars—the administration converted a decade of hard work at restoring fiscal responsibility to ever deepening national

indebtedness. In early 2001 the ten-year budget surplus was pro-
jected to be more than $5 trillion. By dint of tax cuts, a slack
economy, and unanticipated growth in military expenditures,
the 2003 ten-year projection was for a *deficit* of some $5 tril-
lion—a swing of almost $9 trillion, not counting the $4 billion
monthly cost of the continuing occupation of Iraq.[4] Not since
Vietnam had a U.S. administration made the mistake of going
for "guns and butter" simultaneously, or asked so little of an
American people at a time of crisis.

Ordinary Americans could sense the problem, despite record
low interest rates that fueled a boom in housing and refinancing
of residential loans. The unemployment rate crept steadily
upward from the boom times of the Clinton administration.
The loss of some 2.6 million jobs since January 2001 saw the
overall unemployment rate hit 6.4 percent in July 2003—and it
now struck at white-collar, middle-class Americans as businesses
struggled to cut expenses to maintain earnings. And for some
sectors the unemployment was even higher: minorities—youth
under 20, 13.0 percent, young adults 10.3 percent, African-Ameri-
can men, 11.1 percent. Real unemployment, counting those who
had simply dropped out of the labor force, or would have preferred to work if jobs were available, may have been 10 percent or
more. State and local governments were hit especially hard, as
the recession cut their receipts even as the federal government
was attempting to reduce its matching share to many programs.
As states and cities across the country faced local problems of
balancing receipts and expenditures, it was becoming increasingly clear that federal tax cuts either equaled reduced services
and increased unemployment, or offsetting increases in state and
local taxes.

The war on terror greatly compounded the risks we faced. In

the short run, homeland security was underfinanced, denied the resources necessary to prioritize and ameliorate significant risks at home in preventing and responding to terrorism. But also suffering were virtually every domestic program assisted by federal financing: education, health care, and retirement security, as well as the development and refurbishment of infrastructure—programs vital to keeping the United States economically competitive into the future.

Alleviating those risks to our security and prosperity required not stronger rhetoric but clearer thinking. We needed to see ourselves and the world around us in sharp relief—and use that vision better to inform our policies. Simply put, the United States needed a new strategy for the twenty-first century—a broader, more comprehensive, and less unilateralist approach abroad coupled with greater attention to a sound U.S. economy at home, and long-range policies to take our nation forward successfully into the future.

The Bush administration's strategy of preemption, published in the 2002 *National Security Strategy,* was focused against Iraq. At home the formula of the supply-siders—tax cuts for the wealthy to feed trickle-down economics—had about run its course. It was time for America to return to the basic concepts that ensured its unprecedented prosperity and security and to adapt from these a new strategy that can better serve our needs today.

The first of these basic principles should be *inclusiveness.* The United States represents evolutionary values of human dignity and the worth of the individual that have steadily swept across Europe and into much of the rest of the world. We have been proselytizers, advocating our values, assisting states abroad, encouraging emerging young leaders to study and visit the United States and take back their experiences. During the Cold

War we were careful to reach out through the Iron Curtain to the people there. And when the Cold War ended, we worked hard to encourage the enlargement of democracy around the world. We should be seeking allies and friends around the world.

Second, we should be working to *strengthen and use international institutions*, beginning with the United Nations and NATO. Such institutions can provide vital support to American diplomacy, bringing in others to share the burdens and risks that we would otherwise have to carry alone. The UN especially can contribute legitimacy to U.S. purposes and actions. International law is of little significance to most Americans, but it carries heavy weight abroad. Both the UN and NATO need refinement, particularly the UN—but these refinements can be made only through American constructive leadership, for we are the lone superpower with the resources and incentives to do so.

And finally, we must place in proper perspective the *role of the armed forces in our overall strategy*. We should ensure that our armed forces retain the edge over any potential adversary. And they must continue to be modernized to deal with foreseeable contingencies, including the possible need to preempt any threat to the United States. We always have the right of self-defense, including inherently the right to strike preemptively. But force must be used only as a last resort—and then multilaterally if possible.

Operating on these three principles, we should repair our transatlantic relationships. When the United States and Europe stand together, they represent roughly half the world's gross domestic product and three of the five permanent seats on the UN Security Council. These are the countries that are most politically and culturally aligned with the United States. We are the major investors in each other's economies. We should turn upside down nineteenth-century Britain's view that Britain had no permanent friends, only permanent interests. In the West we must have permanent friends and allies and then work to ensure that our interests converge.

Using this transatlantic alliance as our base, we should then work to resolve our security challenges—the North Korean and Iranian nuclear programs, the continuing threat from Al Qaeda and other terrorist groups. We should be working with allies to help settle disputes between India and Pakistan and within the Middle East that could explode into deadly conflict. And we should be pressing through the United Nations and offering assistance to ease the ongoing conflicts in Africa.

In particular, the strategy in the war on terror needed reorientation to focus more on the terrorists themselves and less on the sponsoring states. This meant establishing a tougher network of national and international laws, as well as intelligence and enforcement actions, including appropriate assistance to friendly states around the world to upgrade their abilities to assist us in using law enforcement as the first means of attack against terrorists. We should use NATO to share the burdens of leadership and the UN to reinforce our efforts with additional international authority. And we should open up, not close down, communication with states like Syria and Iran, using all our means and enlisting allies to effect change in policies and activities. In the near term we would have to deepen international engagement in Iraq and Afghanistan, adding to the forces, hopefully with allies, to establish more secure environments and bringing in additional international resources to facilitate political and economic development. We would have to use military force only as a last resort, resisting the temptation to overcommit our relatively limited ground component, dealing more adroitly with historic adversaries in the region, and increasingly using the weapons of law enforcement rather than warfare in attacking terrorism.

Moreover, the strategy needed to focus more on getting at Islamic terrorism's root causes: the extreme Wahhabist ideology and funding from Saudi Arabia; the impoverished, class-ridden, corrupt society of Pakistan and its *madrassas*, and the super-charged linkage with the Palestinians. After the terrorist attacks in June there was some evidence that the Saudi government was looking more seriously at terrorist finance and recruitment, but terrorism's causes are more fundamental, stemming from deep senses of injustice and powerlessness, and the ideology that shapes them toward anger at the West. Thus, winning the "war" required far-reaching reforms in critical societies in the Middle East—more pragmatic education, broader economic development, and wider political participation—as well as the establishment of a just and comprehensive settlement between Israel and the Palestinians. For the United States to effect change in these critical areas would require far more intensive engagement, backed by substantial economic and political development assistance; and given the impact thus far of the U.S. invasion of Iraq, the U.S. would need to provide this assistance through international and regional organizations wherever possible.

We need to put significant resources and a focus of responsibility behind our offers of assistance. The United States needs a cabinet-level or subcabinet-level agency that is charged with developing plans, programs, and personnel structures to assist in the areas of political and economic development abroad. Call it the Department of International Development. Focusing our humanitarian and developmental efforts through a single, responsible department will help us bring the same kind of sustained attention to alleviating deprivation, misery, ethnic conflict, and poverty that we have brought to the problem of warfare. Serious research and development efforts are required to produce technologies, strategies, organizations, and trained personnel who can go into failed states, work with our allies and friends, and promote the political and economic reforms that will meet popular needs and reduce the sources of terrorism and conflict.

Most of our current international institutions are capable and relevant, though they will also benefit from greater transparency and closer attention to the particulars of each country. But we must lead in helping the UN reform itself and adapt to become more useful. We must follow through on commitments. The United States has long been committed to reducing barriers to market flows of goods and services. But we must ensure that trade is both free and fair, helping other nations to meet humane labor standards and reasonable environmental standards.

We also need a new strategy for our nation at home. Success in the war on terror will allow us to face the ongoing economic challenges brought about by our own values and beliefs—an increasingly open international system of trade and commerce, with largely peaceful giant states such as China and India, an increasingly unified European Union, and perhaps other emerging economic centers as well who are sprinting to catch up with the United States. Already, there are several countries, like Germany and Switzerland, whose average standards of living and wage rates exceed our own. These are the special cases: in Germany's case, prosperity through export-led growth directed heavily toward the American market. But the emergence of China and India, as well as an integrated European Union, will mark the first time in American history that we have faced competing integrated markets larger than our own. And even though the U.S. economy today is some ten times larger than China's and almost forty times larger than India's, both nations have increasingly educated and capable workforces, which are already drawing from the United States not only skilled manufacturing jobs but also white-collar and service jobs of the type that were previously considered "safe" at home. Combined with our propensity to spend far more than we save, our long-term economic future is at risk.

In the nineteenth century, we believed in our manifest destiny to span the continent. In the early twentieth century it was to better distribute the power and wealth of America's sudden ascent to major power status—broadening the base of our democracy and using government and labor unions to balance the accumulated private power of great fortunes. But the last third of the twentieth century saw a reaction—a sustained effort to reorder public and private power and responsibilities, reduce the reach of the federal government, and link the interests of the very wealthy to the sympathies of Middle America through tax cuts and the culture war. Now it is time to take stock of where we stand, at home and abroad. We need to redefine our aims as a nation, as well as the strategy and means for reaching them. In the process we need to reaffirm our commitment to the fundamentals of freedom and justice, rights and responsibilities, equality of opportunity and the common good, which have made us a great nation. We need a fresh effort to balance private initiatives and public responsibilities in America, aiming to improve opportunities for all while strengthening American competitiveness for the challenges ahead.

Some problems take a long time to emerge—or to correct. So they have to be worked urgently, every day, even if the payoff seems far removed. Look ahead 100 years, and ask what will we be? In 2103 the United States will be defined by our environment, both the physical environment and our constitutional environment. Today we want to ensure that a century ahead we will remain the most desirable country in the world, attracting talent and investment with the best physical and institutional environment in the world. Environmentally, it means that we must do more now to protect our air, our water, and natural resources, enabling us to extend their economic value indefinitely through wise policies that protect us and the beauty and diversity of our ecosystems—our seacoasts, mountains, wetlands, rain forests, alpine meadows, original timberlands, and open prairies. We will have to balance carefully the short-term needs for commercial exploitation with the longer-term value of the natural gifts our country has received. We may also have to assist market-driven adjustments in urban and rural populations, as we did in the nineteenth century with the Homestead Act.

Institutionally, the U.S. Constitution remains the wellspring of American freedom and prosperity. We will want to retain a pluralistic democracy, with institutional checks and balances to reflect the will of the majority while safeguarding the rights of the minority. We will want to seek to maximize the opportunities for private gain, consistent with concern for the public good. And we will want a civic culture of transparency and accountability, in which we set the world standard for good government. As new areas of concern arise—in intellectual property, bioethics, and other civil areas—we will want to ensure continued access to the courts, and to the other branches of government, as well as a vibrant, competitive media that informs people to enable their effective participation in civic life. And even more important, we will want to ensure that in meeting the near-term challenges of the day—whether they be terrorism or something else—we don't compromise the freedoms and rights that are the very essence of the America we are protecting.

If we are to remain competitive we will have to do more to develop our "human potential." To put it in a more familiar way, we should help every American to "be all he or she can be." For some this means providing a framework of opportunities; for others it means more direct assistance in areas such as education, health care, and retirement security. And these are thirty-year challenges—educating young people from preschool until they are at their most productive; helping adults transition from job to job and profession to profession; promoting physical vigor and good health through public health measures, improved diagnostics, preventive health, and continuing health care to extend longevity and productivity to our natural limits; and strengthening retirement security. We should do these things because it is right for society to reassure all members who have contributed throughout their lifetimes a minimal standard of living, and to free the American worker and family to concentrate on the challenges of today. Such long-term challenges need to be addressed right away, with a new urgency.

We have a solid foundation for meeting these challenges in many of the principles and programs already present today. They need not be enumerated here, except to argue for giving them the necessary priorities and resources. We can never guarantee that everyone has precisely the same education, health care, or retirement security, although we must strive for improvement for all Americans in those areas. But all Americans are better off when we guarantee that each American will have fundamental educational skills and access to further educational development throughout their lives; that each American will have access to the diagnostic, preventive, and acute health care

and medicines needed for productive life, as well as some basic
level of financial security in his or her retirement.

To do this we will have to get the resources and responsibilities
right. In the first place, this means allocating responsibilities
properly between public and private entities. Neither government
nor "the market" are universal tools—each must be used appro-
priately, whether the issues be in security, education, health, or
retirement. Second, we must reexamine private versus public revenues and expenditures. We need greater fiscal responsibility to
balance the federal budget and reduce long-term public debt,
commensurate with immediate economic circumstances, needs,
and priorities—thereby freeing up more capital for business
investment that is required to create new and higher-paying jobs.
And we must ensure that when we run deficits the money is spent
so as to give us the biggest bang for the buck, not the biggest benefit to large campaign contributors. Tax cuts are a good idea, but
we must be certain that we have sufficient funds for defense and
other critical needs. Finally, we need to properly allocate responsibilities among the public and private sectors and among federal,
state, and local entities. This means retaining government regula-
tion where necessary to meet public needs, as well as balancing
the federal government's strengths of standardization and pro-
gressive financing with greater insights into the particular needs
and challenges that state and local authorities bring.

As we work on education, health care, and retirement security we must also improve the business climate in the United
States. This is not simply a matter of reducing interest rates and
stimulating demand. Every year, this economy must create more
than 1 million new jobs just to absorb new entrants to the workforce. To reduce unemployment to the levels achieved during the
Clinton administration, we must do much more. This is in part a
matter of smoothing out the business cycle with traditional

monetary and fiscal tools. But as we improve communications and empower more international trade and finance, firms will naturally shift production and services to areas where the costs are lower. In the near term we should aim to create in America the best business environment in the world—using a variety of positive incentives to keep jobs and businesses here, attract businesses from abroad, and encourage the creation of new jobs, principally through the efforts of small businesses. Employment tax credits for small businesses is one approach. These are not new concerns, but they must be addressed and resourced with a new urgency in facing the increasing challenges of technology and free trade. And the labor movement must assist, promoting the attitudes, skills, education, and worker mobility to enable long overdue rising wages in this country.

Surprisingly, most of the discussions about American Empire—about terrorist threats abroad and our actions to address them—have little to say about America itself. Yet in the wake of 9/11 Americans are seeing themselves in a new way. For the first time in more than a decade, we are aware of the importance of the world beyond our borders, as well as the power of political forces and ideas that aren't our own. And we are looking at each other differently, too, seeking a community with greater trust and security. And we shouldn't believe that we can meet this challenge without ourselves changing in the process.

In the immediate outpouring of international sympathy after 9/11, Americans felt a warmth of support that has seldom been so openly expressed abroad. But much of that sympathy evaporated. Many saw our "fixation" on terrorist threats and claimed their societies had faced this for a generation. But they failed to understand that we are of a different tradition: independent, and determined to restore our sense of security.

The shock, the fear, and the anger will rightly remain embedded in our memories, but now is the time now to "fight smart." It is true that we are engaged in "a campaign unlike any other," and it may well extend for a long time in some form. This is modern war, and no state or society is better able to wage it than us if we will but develop the appropriate strategy and use not just the military forces but also the full array of means at our disposal.

We don't need the New American Empire. Indeed, the very idea of classic empire is obsolete. An interdependent world will no longer accept discriminatory dominance by one nation over others. Instead, a more collaborative, collegiate American strategy will prevail, a strategy based on the great American virtues of tolerance, freedom, and fairness that made this country a beacon of hope in the world.

America's primacy in the world—our great power, our vast range of opportunities, the virtual empire we have helped create—have given us a responsibility for leadership and to lead by example. Our actions matter. And we cannot lead by example unless we are sustained by good leadership. Nothing is more important.

NOTES

Chapter 1: Gulf War, Round Two

1. Woodward, *Washington Post*, March 23, 2003, p. 1.
2. Michael Gordon, *New York Times*, July 20, 2002, p. A1.
3. Conversations, plus Joe Galloway interview with Tommy Franks, *Tampa Times*, published June 2003.
4. Woodward, *Post*, March 23, 2003.

Chapter 2: Rolling North

1. ABC TV, *This Week*, cited in *New York Times*, March 24, 2003, p. 1.
2. *Washington Post*, "Baghdad Hit Hard..." March 28, 2003, p. 1.

Chapter 3: Decisive Operations

1. Scarborough, *Washington Times*, April 9, 2003, p. 1.
2. As this book went to press a secret, draft "Lessons Learned" report, leaked to the *Washington Times* complained of a flawed and rushed postwar planning process, and cited insufficient government assets. See Scarborough, *Washington Times*, September 3, 2003.
3. Priest, *Washington Post*, July 24, 2003, p. 1.
4. Conversation, postwar.

Chapter 4: The Real War: Terrorism

1. Some have tried to link Saddam Hussein to the 1993 bombing—see for instance Laurie Mylroie, *Study of Revenge*, American Enterprise Institute, 2001—but no hard evidence has ever been found.
2. See for example the 1992 draft "Defense Planning Guidance."
3. See *A Clean Break: A New Strategy for Securing the Realm*.
4. Project for a New American Century, letter dated January 26, 1998.
5. Quoted in FAIR-L, *Media Advisory*, "Media Silent on Clark's 9/11 Comments," June 20, 2003.
6. The caller, a Mr. Thomas Hecht, was the founder of the Begin-Sadat Center for Strategic Studies at Bar Ilan University Israel, and Director of its North American branch in Montreal.
7. Woodward, *Bush at War*. New York: Simon and Schuster, 2003, pp. 83–5.
8. Quoted in *New York Times*, September 27, 2001.
9. See UNSCR, 1368 and 1373.
10. Frum, *The Right Man*, chap. 12.

Chapter 5: Flawed Arguments, Flawed Strategy

1. *The National Security Strategy of the United States of America*. Washington, DC: U.S. Government Printing Office, 2002.
2. See Gelman et al., *Washington Post*, August 10, 2003, p. 1.
3. Walter Pincus, *Washington Post*, June 22, 2003, p. A01, one of a series of articles written with Dana Priest.
4. Ashcroft, Statement to the Senate Judiciary Committee, March 4, 2003.
5. *New York Times*, July 14, 2003.
6. Council on Foreign Relations, p. 8.
7. See Aziz Hug, "A Ghost from the Past," *Washington Times*, June 18, 2003.
8. Associated Press, Kathy Gannon, as cited in *Democratic-Gazette* (Little Rock), June 22, 2003.
9. Rumsfeld, Senate Armed Services Committee testimony, July 10, 2003

Chapter 6: Beyond Empire: A New America

1. See, e.g., Robert Kaplan, "Supremacy by Stealth," *Atlantic Monthly*, July 2003.

2. Quoted in Phillips, *Wealth and Democracy*, p. 184, citing Friedman, p. 36.

3. See CBO, *Effective Federal Tax Rates*, Washington, DC, October 2001, p. 134, table 1.2c, as quoted in Phillips, *Wealth and Democracy*, 2002, p. 396.

4. See Richard Kogan, "Deficit Picture Even Grimmer Than New CBO Projections Suggest," Center on Budget and Policy Priorities, 26 August 2003, and "Republicans Oversee Largest Deficits in History: Summary and Analysis of CBO's Economic Outlook," House Budget Committee, Democratic Caucus, August 26, 2003.

ACKNOWLEDGMENTS

I would like to thank the men and women of the armed forces who are the inspiration behind this book and the source of many of its ideas and assessments. Particular thanks go to the dedicated readers and friends who helped me sharpen the thoughts; to the senior officers who cannot be named who corrected the facts; to Dana Priest, Carol Corcoran, Don Epstein, Amy Hunter, and others who read my drafts and helped me set the tone; to my editor and publisher Clive Priddle and Peter Osnos for their understanding, support, and leadership in the difficult process of idea extraction; to my researchers, Jessica Cox and her interns at the Center for Strategic and International Studies in Washington, and Mark Nichols in Little Rock—they were always there for me; to my agent Mort Janklow who helped push me forward; and above all to Gert, who let me sacrifice family time, who was a constant inspiration, whose concern has always been for the welfare of our troops and their families, and the future of the country. Without her, I certainly could not have completed it.

As to the content, the facts, interpretations, and opinions, I take full responsibility.

INDEX

FBI. *See* Federal Bureau of Investigation
Fedayeen Fighters, 19, 44, 52, 61, 64, 79, 80
Federal Bureau of Investigation (FBI)
  intelligence failures and, 141
  war against terrorism and, 127, 143
507th Maintenance Company, 41, 86
15th Marine Expeditionary Unit, 32
1st Armored Division, 25, 26, 87
1st Cavalry Division, x, 25
1st Marine Division, 26, 32–33, 47, 52, 56, 70, 82
floating coalition, 104, 128–29, 152–53
Florida, 122
Food and Agriculture Organization, 181
Fort Carson, Colorado, 25
4th Infantry Division, 22, 25, 26, 65, 83, 84, 87
Fort Hood, Texas, x, 25, 65
Fort Irwin, California, ix, x
Fort Polk, Louisiana, 25
Framework Agreement, 115, 134
France, 51, 107, 164, 185
Franks, Tommy
  assault on Baghdad and, 83–84
  Iraq war and, 34, 59
  plan for Iraq war and, 9–10, 55

G8. *See* Group of Eight
Garner, Jay, 91–92
GATT. *See* General Agreement on Tariffs and Trade
General Agreement on Tariffs and Trade (GATT), 179
Germany, 8, 25, 26, 68–69, 72, 107, 128, 165, 185
Global Hawk, 62
globalization, 180–81
Global Positioning System (GPS), 77
GOP. *See* Republican Party
Gorbachev, Mikhail, 188
GPS. *See* Global Positioning System
Greatest Generation, 160, 165
Greece, 8, 107

Grenada, 188
ground-pounders, 33
Group of Eight (G8), 179
Guantánamo Bay, Cuba, 134

H–2 air base, 33
H–3 air base, 33
The Hague, xi, 100
Haiti, 90–91, 98, 113, 183
Hamas, 130
Hambali, 103–04
Hammurabi Mechanized Division, 40, 58, 70
Hanoi, Vietnam, 33–34
Hellfire antitank missiles, 44
Hezbollah, 130, 134
Hilla, Iraq, 81
Hindayah, Iraq, 64
Homeland Security, Department of, 104, 122, 128–29, 154–55
Homestead Act, 196
Hussein, Qusay, 1, 27, 66, 78
Hussein, Saddam, x, xii
  Al Qaeda and, 114, 134, 146, 159
  American public and, 2
  assault on Baghdad and, 61
  Clinton administration and, 9, 113
  defiance of, 6–7
  deployments by, 84–85
  escape of, 31, 171
  Iraq's WMDs and, 14–15
  Israel and, 5
  Kurds and, 4
  Kuwait invasion of, 140
  lack of compliance of, 23–24
  as mortal threat, 142
  noncompliance of, 113
  Operation Desert Fox and, 7
  Operation Iraqi Freedom and, xi
  Persian Gulf War and, 4
  personal air campaign against, 34, 80
  plan for Iraq war and, 11
  September 11 attacks and, 8–9
  taped messages from, 31, 72–73

PublicAffairs is a publishing house founded in 1997. It is a tribute to the standards, values, and flair of three persons who have served as mentors to countless reporters, writers, editors, and book people of all kinds, including me.

I.F. STONE, proprietor of I. F. Stone's Weekly, combined a commitment to the First Amendment with entrepreneurial zeal and reporting skill and became one of the great independent journalists in American history. At the age of eighty, Izzy published The Trial of Socrates, which was a national bestseller. He wrote the book after he taught himself ancient Greek.

BENJAMIN C. BRADLEE was for nearly thirty years the charismatic editorial leader of The Washington Post. It was Ben who gave the Post the range and courage to pursue such historic issues as Watergate. He supported his reporters with a tenacity that made them fearless and it is no accident that so many became authors of influential, best-selling books.

ROBERT L. BERNSTEIN, the chief executive of Random House for more than a quarter century, guided one of the nation's premier publishing houses. Bob was personally responsible for many books of political dissent and argument that challenged tyranny around the globe. He is also the founder and longtime chair of Human Rights Watch, one of the most respected human rights organizations in the world.

For fifty years, the banner of Public Affairs Press was carried by its owner Morris B. Schnapper, who published Gandhi, Nasser, Toynbee, Truman, and about 1,500 other authors. In 1983, Schnapper was described by The Washington Post as "a redoubtable gadfly." His legacy will endure in the books to come.

Peter Osnos, Publisher